665/3 m

The Nature of Political Inquiry

THE DORSEY SERIES IN POLITICAL SCIENCE

EDITOR NORTON E. LONG *Brandeis University*

The Nature of Political Inquiry

FRED M. FROHOCK, Ph. D.

Assistant Professor of Political Science

Syracuse University

1967

THE DORSEY PRESS • Homewood, Illinois

Library of Congress Catalog Card No. 67–21010

Printed in the United States of America

Preface

This is a book about how we study politics. It deals in values. On these two counts alone it risks the judgment of irrelevance. Certainly no attempt will be made in this work to join the mainstream of modern political analysis with another explanatory theory about politics. But, on the other hand, the areas treated here are part of any explanation, whether recognized or not: epistemological assumptions, explanatory alternatives, science versus intuitive understanding, values in analysis, and so on. What is presented, therefore, is a general sketch of some theoretical questions often taken for granted in contemporary research, but important nevertheless.

The discussion of these topics does not result in a case against observation and experiment in political analysis. Indeed, the book ends with two exhortations for empirical work: a study of socialization in children from precognitive to cognitive stages, and the development of an empirical theory of value for actors in a political system. But the assumption giving cogency to this book is a philosophical one. It is that the reflective scrutiny of theoretical categories can be a valuable analytic task in itself without the burden of gathering data and confirming hypotheses.

Such an assumption amounts to nothing more than what philosophy has been doing since human beings began asking questions about the world. It is still important to reaffirm it every so often, however, for one can easily lose track of the larger picture when filling in the details is so appealing.

Details, to be sure, are necessary ingredients for a comprehensive view. Hence, there will follow in this text no polemic against the establishment of factual generalizations. What *will* follow is a quick, wide scan of some landscape too often overlooked in contemporary political science, with a particular emphasis on values in political investigation.

It will readily become apparent as one reads the following pages that no substantive political theory is discussed. One of the tasks attempted in this book is an identification of certain constant themes in political inquiry. This can only be done at the methodological level. One does not demonstrate a relationship between old and new political theory by juxtaposing relevant theoretical works on pages side by side. The connections (if there are any) are in terms of the way in which politics is studied. Hence, the concentration in the following discussions will not be on *what* a theorist says, but *how* he says it.

I am indebted, as is the case with most authors, to more people than I care to admit for much of what is said in this book. A special thanks must go to Professor James Prothro of the University of North Carolina, who has the supreme gift of a good teacher: intellectual tolerance and appreciation for a wide variety of ideas. Also, I would like to thank Professors W. D. Falk and Maurice Natanson, whose philosophy seminars literally opened up a new intellectual world for me. That this world is still, for me, in the preliminary stages of exploration will be evident in my analysis. I am also grateful to the Social Science Research Council for a grant in Political Theory and Legal Philosophy (1964–65) which made the initial treatment of this subject possible. It is a truism which yet must be stated that none of the preceding individuals or groups necessarily agrees with the ideas in my book, and I hold only myself responsible for its contents. Finally, I would like to thank my parents, Mr. and Mrs. Fred C. Frohock, for providing the financial and personal encouragement to begin and continue my education; and, most especially, my thanks to my wife, whose patience and affection made the arduous task of completing this work a pleasant activity.

Fred M. Frohock

Syracuse, New York
July, 1967

Publication
Acknowledgments

I am grateful to the following publishing companies for permission to quote brief passages from relevant books: Alfred E. Knopf, for a passage from David Easton's *The Political System;* Oxford University Press, for five quotations from Plato's *Republic* (translated by F. Cornford); Humanities Press, for a passage from Peter Winch's *The Idea of a Social Science;* The Noonday Press, for a passage from Jean-Paul Sartre's *The Transcendence of the Ego;* and The Free Press, for a passage from Max Weber's *The Methodology of the Social Sciences.* To the authors of these books I am even more indebted for inspiration over and above the cited selections.

Table of Contents

xi

CHAPTER I

Introduction

What is political inquiry? Or can such a question be asked? In one sense it can be. Whenever we engage in political investigation we are doing something that can itself be an object of scrutiny. If we do not ask what this something is, then we merely take for granted the answer. The question does not disappear. It possesses, in fact, a kind of precedence, for how we study a thing is prior to the conclusions we draw about it. Whether conclusions have validity independent of how they are drawn is itself a part of the same question. No matter how political analysis is sliced, the broad question of methodology cannot be avoided.

But the permanence of this question does not mean that it must yield constant answers. Historical changes in theoretical investigation have been sharp and (seemingly) definitive. Socrates' break with Ionian philosophy is as clear as Hobbes' departure from medieval theory. The current behavioral movement in political analysis has been ascribed the status of a scientific revolution.[1] Yet almost no one would want to argue the extreme thesis that what exists in one historical period is totally unrelated to what has gone on before it. The question is that of discovering the connections, and how tenuous (or strong) they really are.

A task of this sort is a necessary part of defining political inquiry; for inasmuch as the question of inquiry may have different content in accordance with historical periods, a general answer must get at what does not change. Is there, that is, some constant feature of political inquiry, and if so, what is it? If the answer to this question is affirmative, then sharp changes in the history of political thought are all related on the basis of this constant feature. If it is negative, then the question of inquiry is historical only; and any definition of political investigation must be framed within historical conditions.

Two broad categories house whatever definitions can be made of political inquiry. First, political investigation may be distinguished by a certain approach or set of techniques assumed by the investigator. In this case it is the method which sets off political analysis from all other kinds of investigation. Second, the distinctiveness of political inquiry may turn on the subject which is investigated. These two categories—technique and subject—constitute the exhaustive classes by which a discipline may be defined. They may be very closely related in any definition, even to the point where one cannot be defined independently of the other. But no definition of political inquiry can fall outside this typology.

The typology itself is often indicative of one mood or another in political investigation. The scientific climate in modern political inquiry radically separates technique from subject, even to the point where the ideal scientific observer is without subjective location. Classical inquiry, on the other

[1] David Truman, "Disillusion and Regeneration: The Quest for a Discipline," *American Political Science Review* (December 1965), pp. 856–73.

hand, never assumes a sharp separation between analyst and object of investigation. Both share the same purposive framework. But, while the relationship of method and substance varies, the separation is never collapsed. In any inquiry, someone is inquiring and something is being inquired about. To deny this is to deny the investigatory process itself.

THEORETICAL GIVENS

An inquiry into the nature of political investigation is itself vulnerable to queries of method. Because of this, it is necessary to get at the question of presuppositions at the very beginning. Presuppositions will not be avoided in this way; for like Archimedes and his lever, every analyst must have a place to stand. But some reflections are deeper than others; and a philosophical scrutiny of what it is we are doing yields assumptions which might otherwise be missed. This is true even though the scrutiny is itself based on assumptions fugitive to the reflection at hand.

Assumptions may be taken in terms of a continuum from the overt to the unconscious. Some concepts are taken for granted simply for purposes of explanation. An example is the ideal rationality assumed to demonstrate Anthony Downs' model of voting behavior.[2] Such an assumption is recognized; and having been recognized, it may be taken at a later time as problematic instead of given (as indeed it will be later in this work). Some overt methodological assumptions, nevertheless, are so deeply woven into theories that viewing them as problematic alters a whole body of theoretical knowledge. The principle that light travels in straight lines constitutes a given for the entirety of optic theory.

Other kinds of presuppositions are not so overt. Every theory has a tacit dimension which cannot be turned over and peered at whenever we desire. This unconscious part of

[2] Anthony Downs, *An Economic Theory of Democracy* (New York: Harper and Row, 1957).

a theoretical framework is a common feature of our everyday experience. We often realize in retrospect that our reasoning is biased by hidden assumptions which we are not aware of at the time that we argue or judge. Unconscious motivation is so common that it need not be proved here. To deny this kind of tacit dimension is to embrace the absurdity that we know all there is to know about ourselves. The acceptance of covert features is both more modest and more sensible.

Overt assumptions are neither good nor bad. They are simply necessary. Tacit features, however, may assume harmful or beneficial characters. The creative aspects of science have been attributed to the unconscious inclinations of scientists.[3] Gestalt theorists make sense of everyday activity in terms of tacit concepts.[4] On the other hand, error is often a result of the same process. But inasmuch as error is a deviation from intended accuracy, and the intended accuracy is caught up in the same unconscious activity, then we are hard put to separate error from creativity. Perhaps that is why yesterday's scientific mistakes are tomorrow's discoveries.

THEORY AND MODELS

The overt dimension of a scientific theory, formally defined, has these two features: an abstract calculus and rules of correspondence.[5] A calculus is an uninterpreted axiomatic system. Every axiomatic system is comprised of primitive elements (the basic parts of a theory), a set of formation rules (rules denoting how elements are to be organized into legitimate formulations), axioms (the well-formed formulalations resulting from the combination of elements in accord-

[3] Michael Polanyi, *Science, Faith, and Society* (Chicago: University of Chicago Press, 1964).

[4] Wolfgang Kohler, *Gestalt Psychology*. (New York: H. Liveright, 1929).

[5] Ernest Nagel, *The Structure of Science* (New York: Harcourt, Brace & World, 1961), p. 90.

ance with formation rules), and a set of transformation rules (rules denoting how other well-formed formulations, called theorems, are to be derived from the axioms). A formal system of this sort, its symbols not possessing meaning, is a calculus.[6]

An example of an abstract calculus is Euclidean geometry. It is quite possible to manipulate the elements of this geometry in accordance with internal rules without ever assigning any meaning to the symbols being used. Or, put another way, symbols like points and lines have meaning only in terms of the geometrical system of which they are a part. A theory becomes more than a logical skeleton when it is interpreted; that is, when its terms have been assigned meaning outside the formal axiomatic system.

The interpretation of a calculus need not involve the ascription of empirical content to its terms. Axioms of formal systems can be translated into, say, algebraic expressions, in which case the symbols of the calculus are given meaning in terms of arithmetical symbols. But in scientific research the interpretation of a calculus generally means that empirical referents have been assigned to the formal symbols. In such cases we speak of correspondence rules, meaning the set of rules denoting the proper fashion by which the abstract calculus is related to observable events.

Often, but not from necessity, a theory also has a model. A model is, in the most precise sense, an interpretation of a calculus differing from that interpretation which constitutes the theory grounded on the same calculus.[7] Let us say, for example, that an abstract calculus has been developed which is used to represent voting behavior. The representation follows the usual procedure, which is that an empirical theory is drawn from the calculus (thus interpret-

---

[6] For a good brief definition of formal systems and models (to which this section is indebted), see Richard Rudner's *Philosophy of Social Science* (Englewood Cliffs, N.J.: Prentice-Hall, 1966), pp. 10–28.

[7] *Ibid.*, p. 24.

ing it) and this theory is found to be useful in predicting and explaining how people vote. Let us also say that the same calculus can be assigned different empirical terms, such as billiard ball for actor, cue stick for party identification, and so on, and it turns out that the behavior of billiard balls in a game of pool can also be predicted and explained with this alternative theory. Then, *if our primary interest is voting behavior*, the billiard ball theory would be a model for voting behavior. (Of course, if we were mainly interested in billiard balls, then voting behavior would be a model for billiard ball theory.)

An empirical interpretation, in this view, is a model of a theory only if the theory and model share the same logical structure. The advantages in such an overlap are manifold. The entire formal arrangement of propositions in the theory can be discerned with facility if the model is a better-known and better-tested version of the same calculus. Voting behavior, it is safe to say, would be an open book if it shared the same calculus as billiard ball behavior. But if the overlap of calculi is incomplete or nonexistent, then the danger of error cannot be exaggerated. Unfortunately, models are often adopted in the social sciences which are merely common-sense analogies of elaborate theories. When conclusions are drawn in accordance with the model instead of the tested propositions of the theory the results can be disastrous.

In those instances where a common calculus is not a component of a model we do not say that the model is a model *of a theory*. The term may simply denote a physical or abstract representation of phenomena.[8] A physical representation often includes the reconstruction of events using human beings to simulate participation. The reenacting of diplomatic meetings by groups of students and academicians

[8] For this more general approach see: P. Meadows, "Models, System, and Science," *American Sociological Review* 22 (1957), pp. 3–9; J. Beshers, "Models and Theory Construction," *A.S.R.* 22 (1957), pp. 32–38; M. Brodbeck, "Models, Meaning, and Theories," in *Symposium on Sociological Theory*, ed. L. Gross (New York: Harper & Row, 1959) pp. 373–401.

is an example of physical simulation. Abstract representation may range from iconic to mathematical. In neither case—physical or abstract—is an attempt made to construct a microcosm of the phenomena. A model is a reconstruction of salient variables, not a reconstruction of the total universe under concern.

Models, when defined representationally, cannot really be separated from theories except linguistically. Representational models are used in ways which may appear alien to theory-construction, such as teaching and training devices. But the main purposes of models taken in this way are substantially the same as those of any theory: stating lawful relationships between events; providing a ground for making inferences about events; building a body of knowledge; and so on. Further, inasmuch as a representational model must possess a logical interrelationship among its concepts and empirical propositions which are amenable to verification, we have no basis for saying that such a model is anything but a theory.

THEORY: DESCRIPTIVE V. INSTRUMENTAL

Theories have been viewed in one of two ways: either as a description of reality or as an instrument to order experience.[9] The descriptive view of a theory is the older view, and it amounts to the assertion that theories are factual statements about the world which are either true or false. The instrumental position is that theories do not make truth claims about the world, but are frameworks which make the world meaningful. Theories, that is, solve problems as a means of helping us find our way about, but they do not describe things in the fashion in which "X is yellow" describes.

The descriptive view of a theory assumes that any scientific statement can be translated into an equivalent observation statement. Were this not assumed, then no sense could

[9] Nagel, *op. cit.*, pp. 117–52, discusses these conflicting views in depth.

be made out of the assertion that theories describe. Unfortunately for those arguing the descriptive view, such a translation has never been successfully accomplished. One of the reasons for this is the presence of dispositional terms in a theory. Such terms do not describe the features of an object, but rather its behavior under stipulated conditions. One does not, therefore, observe a dispositional feature; one observes (at best) indicators of such a feature.

It is perfectly **proper** to speak of dispositional terms as *never* manifesting themselves. To say that a lump of sugar is soluble is not equivalent to saying that it is dissolved in a liquid, but rather that if it were ever placed in a liquid it would dissolve. It may never be placed in a liquid, and yet still possess the characteristic of solubility. Dispositional concepts would not be a pressing problem for political analysis if such terms were marginal to social inquiry. But many of the key concepts of social inquiry are of this sort, such as attitude, intelligence, and so on. A certain attitude, for example, is often said to exist even though it can be observed only *if* the political actor is interviewed or responds to a questionnaire.

Theoretical concepts which cannot be observed can be gotten at operationally with indicators. The danger is mistaking the indicator for the characteristic. Intelligence, for example, is not merely what is measured by intelligence tests. Many concepts yield an open class of indicators. It would be difficult (continuing the example) to close out definitively the class of activities by which intelligence is represented. The problem is settling on that class of observables which can be taken as the most useful indicator. But in no case can we say that we have observed such concepts directly, nor defined them in any final way.

Only in an instrumental framework can we escape the difficulty of nonobservables. Language itself will not bear the hard requirement that meaningful propositions always ascribe predicates to objects. Many statements are observationals, but a great many others are not. Dispositionals are, in the words of Gilbert Ryle, "inference tickets."[10] They give us the right to make certain inferences about things we experience, even though they do not describe any observable features of these things. At the theoretical level we may accommodate such concepts by viewing theories not as true-false descriptions of the world, but as instrumental tools which permit us to account for our experience.[11]

It makes no sense in the instrumentalist view to search for the existence of theoretical concepts in the world. The proper question is, what can be regarded for physical purposes as a theoretical term? In the case of intelligence, the indicators may be taken for the concept as long as they are useful for making sense of our experience. The question which naturally arises is, how are we to make sense of the world without standards of truth and falsity to guide us? The answer is that truth and falsity can be defined in several ways. The correspondence theory of truth is that sentences describe events, and then are verified in terms of whether or not the events fit the sentences in the way in which they have been described. This version of truth underlies the descriptive view of theories. But we may also speak of truth in terms of the *uses* of sentences. In this view, a sentence can only be judged true or false in terms of the purpose ascribed to it in an experiential context. Does it, that is, help us to do what we intend to do?

What we intend to do is to place in a meaningful framework the events of the world. A theory viewed instrumentally, accordingly, is roughly comparable to a map. It is not a descriptive picture of the world (for a map never purports to represent the totality of any area), but a tool to help us get

[10] Ryle, *The Concept of Mind*, (New York: Barns and Noble, 1964). p. 124.

[11] The most persuasive statement of the instrumentalist thesis is Stephen Toulmin's *The Philosophy of Science* (New York: Harper & Row, 1953). I have relied heavily on his arguments in this section.

where we are going. Insofar as the theory does that, it is a good theory (i.e., "true" theory). Hence, the criteria for adopting a theory are usually these: explanatory power; predictive ability; consistency with other theories already accepted; and intellectual elegance (or parsimony). In no way need we say that a theory describes reality.

One objection to the instrumental account of a theory is that it denies the physical reality of any object postulated by a theory.[12] This misses the point. The claim is that whatever is out there to be taken as reality does not have any meaning until it is subsumed under the rubric of a theoretical scheme. Politics is not politics until it is conceptualized as such, whatever the level of abstraction. Reality v. nonreality is not the issue. It is whether we can know events without a mental framework. The instrumentalist claim is that we cannot. Hence a theory of some sort is necessary in order to get at any reality one postulates; whether this reality exists independent of one's conceptual scheme does not bear on this requirement.

THEORY AS INQUIRY

The question of political inquiry is fundamentally a question of theory. When we investigate something we normally try to explain it, which means that we encase it within one theory or another. Even the identification of facts entails some form of theoretical reference. But all theories are not as tightly woven as established scientific ones. The stipulation earlier that an abstract calculus and rules of correspondence are part of the *formal* definitions of *scientific* theories was no accident. Many commonsense approaches to experience are theories insofar as they adequately generalize a number of events.

[12] Nagel, *op. cit.*, p. 145.

These less formal approaches to the world are not to be summarily dismissed in any discussion of political inquiry. Unlike the physical scientist, the political investigator is faced with subjects who theorize about their world. This means that the study of political events is a secondary abstraction. Actors ascribe meaning to experience; analysts symbolize these subjective meanings at another theoretical level. In a sense the political investigator studies himself, but in another sense he does not. The formal causal frameworks comprising political theory are often at a considerable distance from those meanings constructed by participants in the ordinary world of politics.[13]

One of the reasons for the separation between analyst and actor is the assumption that theory is an objective description of politics. Both normative and historical theory have been subordinated today to causal theory, which in turn is taken as ethically neutral. This is the salient difference between classical and modern political theory. Both Plato and Aristotle incorporate the normative, or *ought*, dimension of politics. Contemporary political inquiry is directed toward describing and explaining the ongoing political system, or what *is* the case. Some modern theorists argue for a general theory of politics to guide and order this research.[14] Others remain content with special theories. But in all cases, theory is taken today to mean the neutral explanatory framework for factual events.

Actors cannot eschew values. Choices must be made and positions defended. Hence political theory will remain distinct from the informal constructions of political actors as long as values are suspended from the investigatory process. If, however, we are to take the instrumentalist argument at

[13] Murray Edelman explores the symbolic meanings of actors in *The Symbolic Uses of Politics*. (Urbana: University of Illinois Press, 1964).

[14] David Easton, *The Political System* (New York: Alfred E. Knopf, 1953).

face value, political inquiry cannot be wholly independent of the *Lebenswelt*. Political theory is that schema which ascribes meaning to the political universe and, as the idealized form of political reality, expresses with exactness those empirical regularities which yield the uniformity of experience. The analyst cannot separate himself from this general experience in an instrumental framework.

The reason for this observation is basic enough. The instrumentalist view moves theory from the object to the subject. In doing so, it makes theory a part of the cultural tradition which has generated the subject; for again, unlike the relationship of a physical scientist to the objects which he studies, the political analyst is part of the empirical forms which he seeks. This observation is not equivalent to the old argument that a social scientist cannot accurately study man because he is himself a man. It is the opposite. Only by dwelling within the conceptual tradition of a polity will an individual have access to the intellectual apparatus which makes political phenomena meaningful. Accuracy is predicated on the framework of tradition.

None of this totally collapses the distinction between analyst and participant. As we shall see, some tension always obtains between these two roles. On the other hand, the neutral scrutiny of politics by independent observers must be severely qualified. It will be the burden of this book to develop and examine the instrumental role of theories as we build a definition of political inquiry. This definition will be developed around the role of values in political investigation; for it is the thesis of this work that the constant theme in political inquiry is the prescriptive behavior found in all political action.

ORIENTATION

The areas to be discussed in defining political inquiry are outlined as follows:

1. The tacit dimensions of theory will be discussed. This will amount to an examination of philosophical frameworks and the methodological possibilities afforded by one epistemology or another. The instrumental function of theories will be elaborated in terms of metaphysical and positivist foundations for political inquiry.

2. The patterns of explanation constituting the *method* dimension of a theory will be examined. Functional and causal analysis will be a special concern inasmuch as they are the two main modes of explanation in political analysis. The problem of *subject* will enter the discussion as the boundaries of political systems are defined. The establishment of criteria for properly functioning systems will demonstrate the necessity of values in functional explanation.

3. The role of science in explaining social phenomena will be examined. This will lead to a lengthy discussion of the differences between physical and social phenomena, and the theoretical approaches appropriate to each kind of data. Whether political inquiry can be a science or not will be answered in terms of an instrumental framework.

4. The question of values in political investigation will be scrutinized. The basic paradoxes of the is–ought schism will be illuminated. The methodological question of a value-free political inquiry will be discussed in the context of a demonstrable distinction between factual and value judgments. A qualified emotivism will be defended as the basis for recommendations in political inquiry.

5. The non-cognitive, or intuitive, foundation of all inquiry will be discussed. The common theme in political inquiry will be identified as an object of study: prescriptive behavior, or the imposition of norms by actors on one another.

Each of the above sets of topics comprises a chapter in the work to follow.

CHAPTER II

Theoretical Givens

PHILOSOPHICAL ASSUMPTIONS

The deepest form of overt assumption is defined as a theory's epistemology. Epistemological statements do not exhaust the premises from which theories are constructed, for the infinite regress of *why* questions in inquiry can also be directed at the philosophical framework itself. The affirmation of an epistemology is itself amenable to queries about validity, or how we come to assume a philosophical framework in the first place. But we can examine our intellectual views of the world which pull up short of a commitment without proof; and, further, the infinite regress which may be directed at all inquiry reveals in itself some of the boundaries and possibilities of investigation.

To begin at the beginning of intellectual discourse entails a consideration of the dialogue between metaphysics and positivism. This kind of exchange may seem to be of more historical than analytic interest, but careful investigation demonstrates the contrary. Inquiry of any sort rests on answers to basic questions of validity, such as what constitutes an adequate explanation and what comprises acceptable evidence. These questions are what metaphysics and positivism are all about; and accepting one or the other approach in political investigation leads to radically disparate conclusions about the nature of inquiry itself.

From these observations it does not follow that one's normative ideas about political systems flow logically from one's metaphysics. They do not. Both Fichte and Emerson shared a similar metaphysic;[1] and both authoritarian and democratic systems have been derived from classical metaphysics.[2] But the disparity *between* positivism and metaphysics does yield contrasting conclusions on the possibilities of politics and, of even more importance here, the possibilities for inquiry into politics. One cannot, after all, begin to form questions and look for evidence until one has settled on some general ideas about what constitutes legitimate questions and answers.

A bothersome issue illustrates this point: can political inquiry be a science? The answer to this query can only be gotten at by unraveling the meaning of science. For better or worse, this meaning is wrapped up in the framework of positivism. No answer, therefore, is possible without a consideration of the general philosophical viewpoint assumed by scientific investigations. Those who dissent entirely from scientific politics fare even less well in escaping the metaphysical dimension of the dialogue. To deny science is itself to rely on extrascientific knowledge. We cannot escape metaphysics and positivism without escaping intellectual discourse itself.

[1] James Ward Smith, *Theme For Reason* (Princeton, N.J.: Princeton University Press, 1957), pp. 39–49.

[2] Thomas Thorson, *The Logic of Democracy* (New York: Holt, Rinehart & Winston, 1962), pp. 44–50.

These two fundamental ways of looking at the world can be defined in terms of what one is willing to accept as the limits of genuine knowledge. Positivism is a philosophy of natural phenomena or, more directly, a philosophy which excludes everything that is not a knowable thing in the sense in which knowable things can be expressed clearly in language. What are accepted in positivism are commonsense explanations of how natural things relate to one another. As one might expect, this locates positivism squarely within an empiricist epistemology. The empiricist position on knowledge is that all knowledge derives from experience, and also that the human mind cannot encounter universals independent of experience.

Metaphysics is based on a different and much larger framework. An explanation solely in terms of natural phenomena is inadequate, although observation is not antagonistic to metaphysics. Metaphysics is concerned with the eternal or essential nature of reality, which leads to such matters as the fundamental causes and processes in things. Again, the point of departure for a metaphysical explanation may be the natural phenomena that positivism ends with, but metaphysics goes considerably beyond the relationship of things apparent to the eye. It is being or existence in the complete sense that is discussed. Accordingly, rationalism is entailed in metaphysics, although all rationalists need not embrace metaphysics. Rationalism is the thesis that the human mind can apprehend universals independent of phenomena, and hence a form of knowledge or set of categories exist which are prior to experience.

One can readily see that a metaphysical approach encounters conceptual problems which are difficult to express clearly in language. This should not be so surprising, for langauge constitutes the intelligible dimensions of existence, and any explanation which goes beyond these immediate dimensions is bound to go beyond the limits of language. For the positivist this is sufficient justification for the elimination of metaphysical inquiry. The metaphysician would argue that, in spite of linguistic problems, his concerns are real ones; and that there is a basic meaningfulness in questions such as: why something instead of nothing?

However one's sympathies are directed, the main difference between metaphysics and positivism is the kind of inference made from that which is experienced.[3] For a positivist, that explanation which can be couched in scientific terms, which generally means subsumed under an empirically verified law, is adequate in explaining the world in which he dwells. For the metaphysician, phenomena seem to require an explanation which goes beyond sensory experience. We can answer the prior question, which is on what basis one infers a little or a lot from phenomena, only by going more deeply into the kinds of philosophical frameworks directing social inquiry.

LOGICAL POSITIVISM

Some justification must be made for a modern criticism of logical positivism, lest the critic be accused of beating dead horses. That the horse is dead cannot be denied, but the specter continues to haunt political inquiry. Again, the tension between a science of politics and a nonscientific view illustrates the relevance of the more extreme versions of logical positivism. In the classic use of the term, objectivity means knowledge which is congruent with a universal referent. For science, objective knowledge is that which has been publicly verified. Put in the context of empirical research, this means that facts are nothing more than the juxtaposition of agreed viewpoints, or conclusions with which any observer would agree provided he follows the same procedure.

[3] Frederick Copleston argues a similar point in *Contemporary Philosophy* (Westminster, Md.: The Newman Press, 1956), pp. 45–53.

The fundamental thesis of logical positivism is that the meaning of a statement is tied to its mode of verification; and, further, that statements which cannot be verified are meaningless. In similar fashion, scientific knowledge is that body of statements verified in accordance with the accepted standards of the scientific community. Any claim not verified has no reason to be taken as true. Hence while the more polemical positions of logical positivism have long been rejected, often by their own adherents, the tie between meaning and verification forms the basis of science. In examining the thesis of logical positivism we are also, therefore, coming to terms with the scientific enterprise.

Further, the peculiarly embracing claims of logical positivism reveal a paradox which holds for all similarly closed claims in an empiricist epistemology. If we move from the assumption that all knowledge derives from experience, then definitive judgments are impossible. The future is open-ended, or tenuous, meaning that one can never rule out the possibility that some later experience may alter even the conceptual apparatus within which arguments take place. Logical positivism does not take into account this limitation. In demonstrating this fundamental error in positivism we are also demonstrating the general boundaries of empirical judgments. This in turn outlines the kinds of moves in political inquiry which are legitimate with an empiricist epistemology.

Finally, the notion that value statements are not verifiable is very much a part of the modern scientific tradition. Naturalism, the older thesis in value theory, was based on the assumption that value statements make truth claims which can be factually validated. With logical positivism we get the emotivist position on values, which is that value statements are merely expressions of feeling; and as expressions of feeling they cannot be said to be generally true or false. It is the emotivist position on values upon which science as a value-free activity rests. Hence the role of values in political inquiry is directly related to the philosophical arguments we are about to encounter.

The most extreme statement of logical positivism can be found in A. J. Ayer's *Language, Truth, and Logic*.[4] Ayer aligns with Hume in asserting that all propositions are either concerned with relations of ideas, or matters of fact. By the former set is meant all a priori propositions of logic and pure math, which are certain only because they do not make assertions about the empirical world. Statements of fact make assertions about observable events, and must be viewed as hypotheses which can be probable, but never certain. This is the classic division between empirical and strictly rational propositions which continues to form a methodological grounding for the physical and social sciences.

Ayer moves this division forward in what he presumes is an elimination of metaphysics. The *coup de grace* is accomplished with the verification thesis of meaning. A factual sentence is said to be genuine only if it is *capable* of being verified by observation; that is, if observation is *relevant* to its truth or falsehood. If this is not the case, then the statement is nonsensical. Further, all genuine statements as defined must then be considered empirical hypotheses, whose function it is to provide a rule for the anticipation of experience.

This meaning criterion reduces all metaphysical statements to nonsense. But it does not rule out a priori statements. Kant distinguished between analytic and synthetic judgments. In the former, the predicate B belongs to the subject A as something which is covertly contained in the concept of A, such as the assertion "all bodies are extended." Synthetic judgments, on the other hand, are assertions of the sort in which the predicate B lies outside the subject A (although it does stand in connection with it), such as "all bodies

[4] A. J. Ayer, *Language, Truth, and Logic* (New York: Dover Publications, Inc., 1952).

are heavy." Kant claimed that knowledge is not extended through analytic judgments, but only rendered intelligible. Ayer follows the main theme of Kant's distinction by allowing two corresponding kinds of validity. A synthetic statement is valid as it accords with the facts of experience, while the validity of an analytic statement depends solely on the definition of the symbols it contains. An analytic statement is not factual, for it only calls attention to the usage of language. Further, Ayer claims, *all* a priori propositions are analytic.

In such a fashion metaphysics is discarded. We need hardly be surprised at this point that Ayer considers Locke's "underlaborer" task the true function of philosophy. This breaks down to demonstrating that observation is the only means of determining truth. Ayer candidly admits that solving the Humean problem of induction is impossible; or, proving that empirical generalizations derived from past experiences will hold good in the future. But for Ayer no alternative exists to empiricism. The philosopher therefore should not attempt to formulate speculative truths, or look for first principles, or make a priori judgments. He should simply confine himself to clarification and analysis in terms of sensation (for material things after all can only be defined in terms of the senses). Put even more briefly, philosophy expresses definitions about the world, or the formal consequences of these definitions.

This thesis leads to a linguistic analysis of truth. Truth and falsity are marks of assertion and denial of a given sentence. The perennial question "What is truth?" is equivalent, according to Ayer, to "What is the nature of X?" This in turn is simply a request for a definition of a symbol in use, which is nothing more than to ask how sentences in which X occurs are to be translated into equivalent sentences which do not contain X or any of its synonyms. This does not deny a congruence theory of truth, for empirical propositions are more or less true according to how they fulfill the central function that they are supposed to fulfill, which is anticipating experience. The validity of the translated statement is the probability that it correctly corresponds to what is observed.

This epistemology leads to a rejection of ethics as a philosophical concern. For Ayer, ethical propositions divide into four main classes. First, there are those that express definitions of ethical terms, or judgments about the legitimacy or possibility of certain definitions. Second, there are those that describe the phenomena of moral experience and their causes. Third, there are those that are mere exhortations to moral virtue. Finally, some statements are simply ethical judgments. Only the first of these types of statements, according to Ayer, can possibly be viewed as ethical philosophy. The second type is merely a branch of psychology, and the last two types of statements are not really statements at all. Ethical judgments, for Ayer, say nothing; they are pure expressions of feeling. Therefore, they are unverifiable. This goes considerably beyond the purely subjectivist notions of normative statements as personal propositions about the speaker's feelings (which would in principle be subject to empirical verification), for what is claimed here is that ethical statements are expressions of feeling which do not necessarily involve any assertions at all. Hence, lacking verification, ethical statements are meaningless.

Logical positivism is a phenomenalistic thesis, since any transcendent reality must be rejected as a prior condition to the discarding of metaphysics. Ayer will not even be pulled into the rationalist–realist tension over the predominance of mind or matter. The sense-contents on which he bases his verification principle are neither mind nor matter, for these categories simply do not apply to the data. The self, in fact, is always reducible to sense-experience, and is nothing more than this. This seems to raise the dilemma of solipsism, which Ayer explicitly realizes. But, he claims, while the other cannot be satisfactorily verified as a subjective unit, still the appearance and behavior of other people make it probable that others exist besides the self.

PARADOXES (I)

The immediate problem with this version of positivism is direct enough: the meaning-criterion postulated is itself not available to the verification procedure which provides for meaning. To make claims of any sort is to assume a philosophical position, and this position must then itself be assumed as true. This requirement does not lead to a paradox when verification requirements are flexible; but when they are drawn rigidly, then the philosophical position constituting the claims in question must be judged by these same requirements. Ayer's logical positivism presupposes a philosophical commitment: the truth of logical positivism. This truth is neither analytic nor synthetic, and thus is not meaningful according to the criterion of the philosophy itself. We have, as a result, no way of defending the principle of verification itself.[5]

But the paradox has a reverse side. The claims of logical positivism are not made meaningless except in terms of an intrinsic standard, the verification thesis, and this standard loses relevance as the paradox emerges. So the claims remain, for what would negate them is itself suspect, though in a more limited way than was intended. They can now be viewed as conceptual distinctions identifying certain kinds of propositions. *All* propositions need not be of one kind or another, even though many might be. The separation in question between analytic and synthetic propositions emerges

[5] This is obviously not a startlingly new criticism, having been made by (among others) J. O. Urmson in *Philosophical Analysis* (Oxford: Clarendon Press, 1956)—although the point is developed somewhat differently in this analysis.

as an ideal scheme, not an epistemological mold into which all knowledge claims must fit.

The source of the verification paradox is not the verification principle itself, but the exclusive manner in which it is drawn up. The theory of meaning in this version of logical positivism categorically denies the securing of legitimate knowledge outside its boundaries. Whenever epistemological limits are severely drawn, the question always arises: are there not experiences (and thus meaningful statements) of a kind quite different from those admitted by the paradigm? No such experience need be explicitly recognized. It is sufficient to see only the limiting requirements themselves, which then as limits suggest an area beyond. In the case of logical positivism, the further question arises: on what basis is the paradigm assumed in the first place? These can remain purely theoretical questions, and still suggest a difficulty for *any* philosophy which draws rigid and closed standards of meaning-criteria.

One escape exists for the problem of grounding the whole of logical positivism, but one should be careful in taking it. An a priori or empirical status can be claimed for the verification principle itself. But, since in the thesis all a priori propositions are seen as tautologies, then the principle can be nothing other than a linguistic rule. Unfortunately, there is no support for its adoption over others except on the empirical basis that it is more congruent with ordinary usage. The possibilities of establishing this, however, are far from certain; and any attempt to bring in such matters as the greater utility or precision of the rule leads into areas very far removed from the limited criteria of the verification principle itself.

Instead of congruency with ordinary usage, just the opposite in fact seems to be the case. It is absurd to suppose that ordinary people generally ascribe meaning on the basis of analytic and synthetic verification. The appropriate bifurcation at this point is between *function* and *verification*. Certainly some meaning accrues from what a proposition does, regardless of its fit within the verification principle. Many terms in language, as we saw in the case of dispositionals, cannot be verified empirically and are not tautologies. Yet they function as meaningful tools in ordinary language. To ignore this is to miss the linguistic foundations upon which all of positivism is based.

Language is a cultural instrument. Its generic development is tied to the experiences people have with one another, and with their physical environment. Even if we suppose the absurd, and hold that meaning and verification are commonly associated, the establishment of empirical propositions occurs within specific experiential contexts. Facts reveal themselves to observers who are located situationally, or within cultural units. This means that as the structure of language relates to experience it is grounded in subjectivity. Transforming language into a systematic form abstracts it *away* from the *Lebenswelt* or life-world of ordinary experience.

Take the statement, "This is a table," as an example. Analyzed systematically, or out of the context in which the statement is used, it is a straightforward empirical assertion. But notice the residue of meaning which is missed when the way that the statement is uttered is ignored: *"This* is a table" or, "This *is* a table" or, "This is a *table*." In every case the emphasis upon one word or another gives the statement a different meaning, none of which can be captured by the verification principle applied to the statement itself. Much of the meaning of the statement is a derivative of its function.

Many supporters of logical positivism have suggested that statements other than those considered genuine by the verification principle are the concern of psychologists and sociologists, and that the focus of philosophy should be upon clarifying language (translating sentences into equivalent sentences) and relating sense experiences to language.[6] To

[6] Ayer himself argues strongly for this in the book under discussion, *Language, Truth, and Logic, op. cit.*

circumscribe inquiry in this fashion, as we have seen, leaves out the nuances of meaning which obtain for men in areas of discourse not considered genuine by the verification procedure (in terms of how they view the world and for what reasons they act in it). Then two questions arise: In what way does this cleavage affect the type of knowledge secured from the vantage point of the verification principle? And what is the advantage to be derived from establishing such a disjuncture?

The advantage is clear: procedural precision is maximized. Going about the business of inquiry is neater when meaning is tied to a dichotomized verification compartment. But refining one's techniques must be weighed in terms of its consequences for the knowledge derived in accordance with these techniques. No possibility exists in the closed statement of positivism for treating the peculiar visions of anyone other than those who are logical positivists. The definition of meaning entails an answer to the further question, meaning for whom? The answer in this case is that meaning is the property of those appropriating the verification principle; and whatever meaning accrues to those outside the boundaries of this approach cannot be dealt with by those within it.

The chasm that has been opened by the verification thesis is that between validated knowledge (as defined) and contextual knowledge. Or, if paralleled with scientific inquiry, between that knowledge held by the analyst and that held by the actor (or participant). The separation is not complete. Scientists, as we shall see, are actors of a special sort; and many ordinary people rely on systematic knowledge. But knowledge which is defined in terms of a strict empirical-analytic verification thesis does not exhaust the knowledge which makes it possible for people to pursue day-to-day activities.

The liability of focusing on linguistic structures alone can be demonstrated again in the positivist thesis on values. Normative and empirical propositions can be distinguished

conceptually as typologies. But, once more, numerous statements are value judgments only on the basis of the context
within which they are made. "He is a Fascist" is a mark of
commendation in Germany during the 1930's, a sign of op-
probrium in today's Western world, and perhaps a description in some earlier historical period. It is the meaning ascribed to the sentence by those using it which determines in
many cases whether the sentence is a value judgment; and
the hard distinction between value and fact cannot be maintained by investigating the sentence itself.

Even when we can readily identify a value proposition out
of context, such as those sentences containing a categorical
good, no form of verification is allowed to such judgments in
the positivist thesis. Hence they are meaningless. But, once
more, the severity with which the thesis is drawn reiterates
the separation between the analytic scheme and the subjective meanings of actors. Human beings make choices, many
of which are based on values. That those values may be emotional commitments of a fundamental sort does not obviate
the fact that meaning is ascribed to values by actors in a
way that is independent of the verification thesis. Failing to
take these into account removes positivism from the area of
commonsense activity, a place where the origins and full
meanings of language are housed.

What is missing in an inquiry based on positivism is a feel
for the relational patterns of human life. The cutting edge of
the verification thesis, strictly defined, becomes paradoxical
again in the self–other relationship. Ayer's proof of the existence of the other is no real proof at all, but only an inference
from analogy. The problem of solipsism may yield only to
inferences instead of definitive attacks. But this poses a peculiar problem for the verification principle. Verification
means a general proof, or the confirmation of some claim
by at least two people. There can be purely personal verification, as when we are satisfied that some set of conditions
or type of statement has met with certain of our qualifying

standards. But this is not the way that the term is used in logical positivism. A principle is established for a more universal judgment of propositions, meaning that anyone adopting the principle can secure results similar to those obtained by others. The verification principle, that is, is a general analytic tool. But propositions can only be so verified if others exist; and since others exist only problematically, then the verification possibilities of logical positivism can only be problematical, and not certain.

All of the difficulties demonstrate the malaise of empiricism when empiricism is taken to its logical extremes. Positivism results in a contradiction when it is presented as a closed claim. The contradiction, in turn, ensues because of the empirical asumption about what we can know, which is that all knowledge derives from experience. Given this assumption, only open-ended (or tentative) claims are possible. Experience, as the basis for knowledge, is not only vulnerable to distortion but also subject to the perennial contingency of the future. Such a foundation disallows the rigid certainty ascribed to the verification thesis. To establish that degree of certainty would entail an intuitive truth or extraexperiential standard, which is excluded in the empiricist approach. Skepticism, for the positivist, must be its own reward.

PARADOXES (II)

But, as we might expect, skepticism has its liabilities as well. Positivism is not the whole story of empiricism. As a special, and extreme, case, it denotes some of the problems awaiting extravagant claims made from modest premises. But a more general problem plagues empiricism, which is that knowledge derived from experience is relative to experience, and hence not of universal validity. To get away from relativism is impossible in the empiricist framework, for we would expect experience (and hence knowledge) to differ in accordance with time and circumstances. The *tabula rasa* fills up capriciously, the anthropologists tell us, and with many things. To a world accustomed to relativity in physics, this entailment may seem something less than a problem. But, as we shall see, it poses a peculiar dilemma.

The implications of relative knowledge are treated at length by Karl Mannheim in *Ideology and Utopia*.[7] Mannheim's thesis, loosely captioned "the sociology of knowledge," is that there are modes of thought which cannot be adequately understood as long as their social origins are obscured. This is a lesser claim than the assertion of total relativity, and, we would expect, one that should be easier to defend. But, as with Ayer, the only type of knowledge which Mannheim accepts as universal is analytic, or the systems of logic and mathematics which do not depend for their validity upon their surrounding worlds. Nor does Mannheim ascribe too much importance to this type of knowledge. Certainly he does not hold it relevant to the acute problems of human behavior, which he holds are inextricably lodged in perspectives of some sort.

For Mannheim, certainty of knowledge about the world is impossible because of the way in which knowledge comes about. Normally, epistemology explains meaning from its genesis in the specific subject. But in Mannheim's thesis the individual mind cannot be conceived of as separate from the group. Knowledge is a cooperative process of collective life. This means that knowledge is conditioned by social forces. It also means that the very condition for the existence of knowledge is the field of cultural forces acting upon the individual.

New forms of knowledge grow out of the conditions of collective life, and do not depend for their emergence upon the prior demonstration by a theory of knowledge that they are possible, or efficacious. Hence, developments in epistemology are always sequels to developments in the immediate

[7] Karl Mannheim, *Ideology and Utopia* (New York: Harcourt, Brace & Co., 1936), p. 293.

empirical procedures for getting knowledge. What is generated substantively in social change is itself the ground for perspectives and commitments constituting the basic framework of knowledge. In this fundamental sense, there exists a nexus between epistemology and the general sociointellectual situation of an historical period.

This does not in itself deny objectivity, but it gives it a modern twist. For one thing, of course, two-plus-two equals four no matter what the social climate; but, again, neither does this reveal anything significant about the human condition. However, if objectivity is taken to mean a generally accepted truth instead of a general truth, then objectivity is possible within Mannheim's philosophy. That is, insofar as different observers are immersed in the same system they will, on the basis of the identity of their conceptual apparatus expected from their common universe, arrive at similar results. Of course, subjects within different systems can share verification only in random fashion.

Mannheim is fully aware of the dilemma central to the relativist and, as we have seen, to the positivist: the subjection of his own assertions to the same claims. For this reason, Mannheim will not allow his thinker to grasp any rigid standard. Instead, he constructs an escape for the problem which does not exclude evaluations, but is in fact based on a critical awareness and control of them. What Mannheim suggests is that the philosopher may become a mobile critic, incorporating points of view in order to reveal more fully the basis of his own perspective. Instead of trying to secure an impersonal objectivity (which is in Mannheim's view impossible and thus a source of error), the theorist enlarges the validity of his own conclusions by recognizing and juxtaposing his own and other's viewpoints. Awareness of subjectivity is the means for overcoming distortion.

❖   ❖   ❖   ❖

Does this peculiar awareness succeed? It does not seem so. As another critic has pointed out, it resembles Munchhausen's feat of extricating himself from a swamp by pulling on his own whiskers.[8] The sociology of knowledge is presented as a universally valid proposition, but the substance of the thesis is that there are no propositions which totally escape the relativity of circumstances. If this paradox seems familiar, we shouldn't be surprised. Once more we have the inappropriate marriage of a closed claim (*all* knowledge) with an assertion of contingency (is culturally *relative*). No amount of maneuvering can evade this paradox.

Even the universality of tautologies breaks down in Mannheim's thesis. Once established, tautologies are true by virtue of their internal consistency. But within the framework of the sociology of knowledge, the very terms and rules by which tautologies are accepted would be themselves grounded in the relationship human beings have with each other, and with their physical environment. The axioms of, say, mathematics cannot be validated outside of cultural circumstances. It would appear, in fact, that axioms and symbolic operations are established as logical antecedents on the prior assumption that mathematics is valid. Mathematical conclusions are, after all, only as true as the premises from which they derive.[9] Even a pragmatic defense of mathematics suffers from cultural relativity, for any criterion of utility must be defined within one perspective or another.

On top of the internal contradiction is a difficulty which would make the sociology of knowledge thesis meaningless regardless of the relativity paradox: the inadequate construction of the argument. Simply to claim that knowledge is conditioned by cultural forces is similar to the classic economic qualification "all other things being equal." Unless such qualifications are specified, the claim in question can never be refuted. More is involved here than making a thesis

[8] Robert Merton, *Social Theory and Social Structure* (Glencoe, Ill.: The Free Press, 1957), p. 507.

[9] This observation is part of Michael Polanyi's case for tacit knowledge. Polyani's most comprehensive statement for tacit knowing is in his *Personal Knowledge* (Chicago, University of Chicago Press, 1958).

operational. The problem is that Mannheim's thesis is empirical, and thus requires a specification of the factual conditions under which it is more or less pronounced.

This requirement means that the actual relationship between various cultural conditions and certain conceptual positions must be explicitly indicated. Otherwise, the claim is vacuous; and, if vacuous, any denial that idea X is a result of cultural forces can be dismissed out of hand by adherents of the sociology of knowledge. This amounts to the absurdity that empirical instances do not bear upon the validity of an empirical concept. What is needed to avoid such intellectual poverty is a factual elaboration of Mannheim's thesis. Unfortunately, the grandiosity of the thesis makes exhaustive validation an impossibility.

All of this simply indicates again the impossibility of securing universally certain knowledge in the empiricist framework. Without a standard independent of circumstances, knowledge is the victim of circumstances. One can appreciate Mannheim's assumption of a negative position which unveils facades, glimpsing (hopefully) in doing so one's own role as unmasker of perspectives. But, as we have seen, it does not work, for revealing one's own *Weltanschauung* requires a position outside of experience. Adopting Mannheim's thesis entails the surrendering of certain knowledge, and thus even the certainty of the sociology of knowledge. This is the specter which haunts all empiricism.

CLASSICAL THEORY

For Aristotle, metaphysics is the first philosophy, or that intellectual activity which focuses on the essential and unchanging nature of being. Metaphysical inquiry as the pursuit of fundamental structures is even more central to Platonic theory, for Plato's theory of forms constitutes the stable reference explaining all of existence. We can see immediately that the skepticism needed to keep positivism from contradicting itslf is alien to the classical concern with things which are not contingent. Further, by not restricting the scope of knowledge to sensory experience in the way that modern empiricists do, we will discover that the kinds of difficulties found in positivism, and hence in modern science, do not obtain for classical thought.

But all of this would be posed too easily if we conclude that the classical framework solves (by not considering) the problems coming out of empiricism. A problem is, inextricably, a part of the theoretical framework adopted, but theoretical frameworks are adopted for reasons other than the fact that they do not embody certain thorny problems. One thing that a theory does is explain things, and to increase explanation may often mean assuming the burdens of one dilemma or another left out of a schema with less explanatory power. The scale for assessing theories may be balanced in accordance with several standards, including the continuum from explicit to tacit truths. A sketch of the differences between ancient and modern inquiry will demonstrate this particular scale.

In Platonic thought knowledge must be both *true*, and of what *is*. If we know something, the question of error is not a possibility. All knowledge, in fact, is knowledge of fixed structures, for nothing *is* except that it does not change. This definition of knowledge is wholly antagonistic to empiricism, for Plato denies both the circumscription of knowledge to experience and the notion that experience is any way the source of knowledge. Perception, in the Platonic framework, can never be the basis of knowledge; for what we perceive empirically changes, and what changes cannot be known.

But the Platonic case against the more extreme versions of empiricism rests on an even broader foundation than that of stability v. change. Even if phenomena were somehow stable, the problems of perception would remain in Plato's philosophy. What we see and hear and feel, finally, is situationally located. Truth for one man may be error for another. Put in a later terminology, the facticity of individual location allows us to see only adumbrations, or splinters, of the surrounding world. This partial seeing from the physical locations of our bodies still could only be called knowledge in the Platonic schema at the actual time of perception, for memory is not infallible.[10]

Even within the limitations of one's own perceptual sphere, according to classical standards, one cannot know the facts simply from the facts. A mental referant is always needed. To know the truth about what we encounter in experience entails reflection about such matters as the source of an object's existence and its similarity to other things, all of which lead beyond immediate perception.[11] So far, this part of Plato's argument is familiar enough. Certainly neither Ayer nor Mannheim would dissent from it. The crucial differences occur in what one is to make of these obvious limitations, and if one is to try to overcome them.

The characteristic feature of empiricism is to stay within the imperfections of sensory experience. Plato does not do so. He argues that judgments of knowledge are really judgments which focus on universals. A judgment that something is X really means that this kind of thing is X. For Plato, this suggests that knowledge is really about objective universals which are distinct from sensory things. In contrast to Aristotle, he argues that these objective references are independent of phenomena. The empirical world is an imperfect reflection of the objective world of forms, which is true reality and the subject of all knowledge.

The particular things which we apprehend through our senses cannot, Plato argues, be known as specific objects. We know specific things only as they participate in the generality of the form. Since we know only in terms of universals, what is wholly specific is wholly unique, and thus unknow-

---

[10] *Theaetetus.*
[11] *Ibid.*

able. Empirical objects are therefore both real and intelligible to the degree that they *approximate* the forms. Emphasis must be given to the idea of approximation, for phenomena are never instances of the forms inasmuch as the forms are transcendent in Platonic theory. What *is* the case for Plato is an objective reality separate from experienced things.

The separation between forms and sensible things is not a physical one in the normal use of the word. One is tempted to say that it is a conceptual separation which is meant, but this won't quite do either. The problem is that the very dimensions of space and time are inappropriate in discussing the forms, and so we must get away from the bizarre idea that the forms occupy a physical place of some sort. On the other hand, we must not see them exclusively as mental referents, for they constitute being, or reality, in Platonic theory. Forms exist independently of the sensory world, but their existence is beyond the boundaries of normal description. This is the source of the difficulty in explaining the existence of the forms: explanation must be couched in language, which remains within the sensory world.

From this account, it follows that knowledge cannot be derived from experience in the Platonic framework. We come to know only through an intellectual process that is essentially internal, and divorced from sensory data. Mathematics and logic are the beginnings of cognitive awareness. In higher stages of learning one focuses on the principles from which deductive reasoning moves. The intellectual process constructed by Plato is a progressively abstract examination of assumptions. Available to a few individuals is the form which unifies the premises of all knowledge: the Good. From this highest form the unity of both the epistemological and ethical dimensions of the world derive. Knowledge, ethics, and existence are joined.

Aristotle is often posed as the empiricist who contrasts with Plato's idealism. The differences between these two classical thinkers is considerable within the classical framework, but not nearly so great when both are compared to modern thought. We may say, in fact, that taken together they constitute the boundaries of classical thought as it contrasts with modern inquiry. Both, most especially, make the strongest of cases for certain knowledge in opposition to relativism. The world is seen in terms of a universal structure which gives meaning to judgments of both ethical and knowledgeable import.

As classical theorists they differ. The first significant dissent from Plato's theory of forms comes from Aristotle. For Aristotle, universals are immanent, not transcendent. To separate them from objects is, in his view, simply impossible. However, Aristotle still views universals as objective. What he claims is that forms can only be the common features which things share, and which accordingly make them intelligible. But to abstract these universals to an independent sphere is to ignore the fact that they can exist only in terms of empirical properties. Even in the abstract sphere of mathematics, Aristotle holds, symbols are simply conceptualized representations of physical objects, and depend for their existence on these objects.

The earliest version of the third-man argument comes from Aristotle. This is the criticism that the Platonic separation of the forms from the objects engenders the need for a third form to link the initial form and the object, which in turn necessitates another set of forms to establish the relationship between the third form on the one hand, and the first form and the object on the other, and so on down an infinite regress. The basis of this criticism is that if forms represent the similar features of objects, then a comparable similarity obtains between the independent form and the object which approximates it, thus necessitating a third form, ad infinitum. This entire morass of how an object participates in a form which exists separate from the object is escaped by Aristotle's doctrine of immanence.

But to say of universals that they are empirical is not tantamount, in Aristotelian thought, to saying that they are either factual contingencies or constructs of the mind imposed on phenomena. For Aristotle, factual assertions can be certain, not probable; and this certainty is a feature of the world's structure, which imposes itself on the mind. We do not create order; we apprehend order. Hence, the Aristotelian universals are grasped inductively by the intellect. This formulation of induction is alien to the positivist mood, which allows (as we have seen) for analytic certainty but factual probability only. In Aristotelian thought, however, one can by observing the facts apprehend and exhibit the intelligible structure of the facts. Aristotelian science is a deductive demonstration from such inductively derived principles.[12]

For both Plato and Aristotle, but especially for Aristotle, the modern cleavage between analytic and synthetic propositions is not pursued. The structure of the Greek language parallels, for Aristotle, the structure of the world. Hence, analytic statements are also factual propositions. The structure of language also yields the nature of reality for Plato, except that reality is never the sensory world, nor is it exhausted by ordinary language. But, for Aristotle, to know a thing entails expressing it in language; and the nuances of the world are related in terms of logical, or linguistic, structures. Nor, we might add, is the separation between statements of fact and statements of value so harshly drawn for classical thought as is the case in positivism. For both theorists, a standard of knowledge is the source of validation for norms. In classical value theory and theory of knowledge, objective standards exist, the one to say what is right and the other to say what is wrong; and neither kind of standard is divorced from the other.

Experience, in Aristotelian theory, can however be a source of knowledge. But Aristotle's notion of experience is diametrically opposed to that of the positivist. That which we

[12] John Randall, *Aristotle* (New York: Columbia University Press, 1960), pp. 1–58.

grasp through our senses is not, for Aristotle, James' "booming, buzzing confusion," but rather a completely intelligible world which constitutes the dimensions of the intellect. The object known is like a stone pressed into the clay of the mind; the content of the mind *is* the world as known. For Aristotle, no mystery surrounds the process of knowing the world. It is simply an accomplished fact.[13]

The Aristotelian depiction of experience is also contrary to Plato's emphasis on independent forms. But, again, these contrasts can be overdrawn if we forget the differences between both these classical theorists and modern inquiry. For Plato, what *is* the case is the forms; experience is authentic as it embraces the forms. The sensory world is contingency. Aristotle's reality is the everyday world, which is the source of certain knowledge. The reality of experience in positivism is the sensory world, but without Aristotle's universals or Plato's forms. What is real is certain for both classical theorists; what is real is probabilistic for positivism.

Again, Aristotle at no time argues the intellectual unity which Plato constructs. Each subject amenable to study has, for Aristotle, an appropriate mode of inquiry. As indicated earlier, metaphysics focuses on the first principles which give meaning to the sciences. Mathematics treats motionless objects abstracted (but not separated in existence) from phenomena. Physics explains motion. But what contrasts all intellectual approaches within Aristotelian thought from the practical sciences, and outside Aristotelian thought from contemporary positivism, is the Platonic notion of standards which are of universal validity.

One brief word must be said about the kinds of knowledge distinguished in Aristotle's philosophy. Theoretical wisdom is constituted by knowledge which is pursued for its own sake, and is focused on the necessary. Practical and productive knowledge are means (respectively) to conduct and to the

[13] *Ibid.*

making of that which is useful or beautiful. What may appear to move Aristotle closer to modern inquiry than we have made him out to be is the fact that the focal point of practical wisdom and art is that which is contingent.

Two observations demonstrate why we must leave Aristotle where we have placed him. First, in any contingent situation the presence of an internal standard—which is reason itself—yields the end, for Aristotle, to which any activity must be directed. Thus contingency cannot mean caprice. Second, while circumstances must be taken into account in determining the norms of practical science, circumstances are not so very different in Aristotle's view. To be relative to time and place is, for Aristotle, to remain generally similar. The cultural diversity of Mannheim's world is not countenanced by either classical theorist.

KNOWLEDGE AND ONTOLOGY

From this brief account we can see how the classical case for knowing the world, and what kind of world there is to be known, differs from positivism. In spite of the well-known distinctions between Plato and Aristotle, both develop epistemologies grounded in certain knowledge. For Plato, the source of this knowledge is a transcendent form independent of the sensory world. Aristotle derives the forms from experience. But in both cases standards of correctness are available to the human intellect which are universally true. Plato and Aristotle are rationalists, then; in the sense that they claim for the mind an ability to apprehend essential structures.

But, as we have indicated, the problems of empiricism are not voided without the assumption of other difficulties. One remarkable feature of the highest Form in the *Republic*, the Good, will indicate what these difficulties are. In spite of the fact that the Good is the ultimate source of knowledge, in no part of the dialogue is this Form precisely explained. So Socrates tells Glaucon that

. . . just as in our analogy light and vision were to be thought of as like the Sun, but not identical with it, so here both knowledge and truth are to be regarded as like the Good, but to identify either with the Good is wrong. . . . Goodness is not the same thing as being, but even beyond being, surpassing it in dignity and power.[14]

Even the process by which the Good is grasped is explained indirectly. Plato here uses the allegory of the cave, again using the sun as a rough analogy for the Good.

Last of all, he would be able to look at the Sun and contemplate its nature, not as it appears when reflected in water or any alien medium, but as it is itself in its own domain.[15]

Later, the function of the Good is more directly indicated, although its meaning still remains obscure.

In the world of knowledge, the last thing to be perceived and only with great difficulty is the essential Form of Goodness. Once it is perceived, the conclusion must follow that, for all things, this is the cause of whatever is right and good; in the visible world it gives birth to light, while it is itself sovereign in the intelligible world and the parent of intelligence and truth. Without having had a vision of this Form no one can act with wisdom, either in his own life or in matters of state.[16]

The significance of this Form perhaps will excuse the length and frequency of these quotations, for what is at issue here is a truth which cannot be talked about in ordinary language, and yet which functions as the universal standard for ethics and knowledge. Much can be made of this, and has been, in ascribing authoritarianism to Plato.[17] But the

[14] *Republic*, trans. Francis Cornford (New York: Oxford University Press, 1945), p. 220.

[15] *Ibid.*, p. 230.

[16] *Ibid.*, p. 231.

[17] See, as the representative work, Karl Popper's *The Open Society and Its Enemies* (Princeton, N.J.: Princeton University Press, 1963).

purpose in bringing up these passages from the *Republic* is not to inquire into the perennial problem of Plato's nondemocratic proclivities. Of more interest are the burdens which must be assumed conceptually if we are to affirm the Platonic framework.

Why the Good is opaque is obvious enough. By definition, any concept which transcends ordinary things goes beyond the dimensions of language (and hence of communication). But however clear this is, the effects of such a move remain definitive in the other direction. Only a few individuals can ever apprehend the Good, and only as the result of an intuitive, and therefore highly personal, experience. This means that the correct standard which circumvents the contingency of empiricism is fugitive to most men, and (at best) private to a few. The relativism characteristic of empiricism is safely discharged in classical theory, but the explicitness of empirical inquiry has vanished. What has been sacrificed to gain certainty is lucidity.

The response to all of this may be that we are taking Plato at his mystical worst. In the earlier dialogues the clear skepticism of Socrates is very much present, as it is in the first parts of the *Republic*, where Plato argues for a standard of correct knowledge which amounts to little more than internal reflection prior to acting.[18] This is true, and even more relevant to Aristotle, who nowhere descends to obtuseness when constructing the first principles of knowledge. But even though rationalism can be separated from mysticism, the explicit dimensions of classical theory rest on assumptions considerably less visible than those grounding positivism.

Rationalism, whether classical or not, assumes a priori knowledge, which may be taken to mean some substantive

[18] This is true in spite of the fashionable attempts to make both Socrates and Plato fit certain modern views more religious than philosophical. See, as characteristic of these attempts, Eric Voegelin's *Order and History*, Vols. II and III, (Baton Rouge: Louisiana State University Press, 1957).

or mechanistic framework which is independent of experience. For both Plato and Aristotle (leaving out the obvious mysticism of the later Platonic dialogues), that standard which holds regardless of circumstances is reason itself. As a static feature of human nature, reason is mechanistic for both theorists. Man is distinguished from other animals by his ability to reflect, and not by his capacity to align with any substantive norms (although reason will lead toward certain values). But the basis for this universality, in both classical thinkers, is a peculiar assumption whether reason is defined mechanistically or substantively. It is comprised of one (or both) of two views: either we all come to terms with the world in the same way, or the world is presented to us in uniform fashion.

The problem suggested here is this: To argue that all knowledge derives from experience, as the empiricist does, leads normally to relativism. This is clear from the earlier discussion of Ayer and Mannheim. One can escape this in the classical approach by relying on a universal standard, which both Plato and Aristotle do. But the source of this standard must be either in the mind or in the world, and in either case it opens the door to considerable difficulty. If it is posed as a structural part of the world, to be encountered by human beings who do not in themselves possess an ordering faculty, then the problem of defining the standard arises. Without the capacity for order, we would expect each person to encounter structures differently, and we are back once more to Plato's criticisms of subjectivity. To define universal structures without making assumptions about those who grasp them is (unavoidably) to move these standards within subjective fields, at which time they become personal and no longer universal.

No rationalist is so foolish. Whatever the postulates about the world, assumptions are always made in rationalism about the capacity of the human mind. Certainly Plato and Aristotle, as we have seen, stipulate a rational faculty common to all men. In the general sense of rationalist assumptions about the mind, such an a priori framework can mean either substantive knowledge or a categorical mechanism. In the first sense, the claim is that we are born with fundamental knowledge of one sort or another. Plato argues a version of this in the *Republic*. In the second sense, the faculties of the mind are said to encounter experience in a way common to all men. The intellect, in Aristotelian theory, is universal in this way.

But whichever assumptions one aligns with, the question arises: what is the source of this a priori framework if it is not the knowable world? Plato argues that its source is what we really are in the first place; learning is a discovery of the self. But this is hardly a satisfactory answer, for one must specify the origin of the self if it is not to be the experience of life. It may seem, of course, that this line of inquiry can also be made to apply to positivism, for questions about the origin of experience certainly are not answered by empiricists. But the crucial thing here is that empiricism stays within experience, whatever the liabilities of this, and thus does not incorporate into the explanatory scheme assumptions which point directly to origins.

A balance between the tacit and the overt (we will recall) is operative in any theory. Theorizing entails taking some things as unproved. What is taken as a given, and in what way, is the issue separating empiricism and rationalism. The given in empiricism is methodological only, or what is minimally needed for purposes of the analysis at hand. One may object that more baggage really comes along in practical pursuits than this conceptual ideal indicates or that empiricism may be pushed back to more fundamental givens, but this is another matter. It is the *conceptualization* of rationalism which yields a broader area of the tacit. The given for the rationalist is an assumption which can never be brought to the surface; as the condition for experience, it must remain fugitive to experience. Also, the rationalist's a priori is not a methodological device, but general truths about the world and those who live in it.

One can see that no answer can be made to the queries

about the origins of these truths, for any appropriate answer would be outside experience and therefore not intelligible. These things simply have to be assumed as part of the rationalist framework. This does not in itself constitute a problem, for problems can only be defined within one framework or another, and one may simply affirm these truths without difficulty. But we should understand that the classical framework escapes the dilemma of relativism only by assuming a number of substantive givens, beyond explicit proof even within classical thought, and we should be prepared to accept them *without proof* if this alternative to relativism is adopted. Certain knowledge does not come without its own peculiar burdens. In this case, these are a considerable expansion of the covert areas of theory.

NATURAL LAW AND RIGHT

The notion that a structural reality exists from which to deduce certain knowledge, as well as a capacity on the part of human beings to discover universals, is one which begins but does not end with classical philosophy. Both a religious and a secular tradition can be distinguished within this one theoretical framework. Not so surprisingly, the source of the rationalist a priori for theologians is God. Not all theologians are rationalists, of course, anymore than all rationalists are theologians. But a coupling of reason and revelation within a single approach is very much in the tradition of medieval philosophy. To attempt to trace either the secular or the religious tradition in rationalism would be a separate work in itself. It is sufficient to realize that both the theological and the temporal can be gotten out of classical theory. All one has to do is try hard enough.

The secular emphasis is of more interest because it leads to natural law in political philosophy. All secular natural law theses assume that standards exist which are true regardless of circumstances, yet which are not derivative of divine ordinance. But, while revelation does not play a part in originating these universal norms, a universally believed standard is not necessarily natural. Acknowledgment is neither a necessary nor a sufficient condition for natural norms. So while God does not create natural standards, neither, strictly speaking, does man. True regardless of circumstances means true regardless of the dictates of God *or* man.

The standards fundamental to natural law are the source of both knowledge and ethics. The meaning of the world is also a prescription for the behavior of men. For this to be otherwise would be impossible. The objective reference in natural law is, with respect to the human condition, a definition of the essential nature of men. To be wise is to know the standard; to be good is to act in accordance with it. So while the question of values will be discussed at greater length later, the use of norms in discussions of natural law denotes both an epistemic and normative directive.

On the character of the natural order, or structural reality, natural law theorists disagree. The two main positions on the issue may be roughly traced back to Plato and Aristotle. In Platonic thought the source of knowledge is a stable referent. An unchanging structure, as we have seen, also constitutes the basis for Aristotelian metaphysics. But Aristotle also allows for genuine knowledge of change. The physical world, for Aristotle, moves toward fulfillment, which is the realization of each object's final end. This teleological process is not a conscious one except in man. But neither is it random. An end-state consists of what an object essentially is, in the sense that a thing is potentially what it is to become. Both Platonic stability and Aristotelian teleology have been adopted as differing characterizations of the natural order of things.

The Aristotelian version is more loosely defined. Within a teleological framework, the total existential situation is usually considered the origin of natural law, and this includes both subject and object. In fact, this very division between subjective and objective categories is somewhat misleading, for the situation collapses perceiver and perceived. Both observer and object possess natural ends. In some teleological theories ends are incomplete in any given situation, and existence has no determinant properties. The world is dynamic, and obligation comes about from the nature of this process. What is implied are modes of existence, instead of determinate structures, and any impediment of these fundamental tendencies is evil. Goodness is the fulfillment of being, or the completion of existence.[19]

Obligation in these naturalistic terms is coincidental with a subjective feeling of "ought" which comes about from the tendential state of being. We feel compelled to fulfill ourselves. This does not mean that every desire is naturally right, or even instrumental to fulfillment. A distinction still holds between good and bad compulsions. But the exact nature of this distinction can only be determined with knowledge of the natural end of man. All natural beings have an end, and man (as part of the existential situation) has his own distinctive purpose also. So what *is* the case is not entirely identified with what *ought* to be, but the norm which reveals the ethical development of phenomena is found within the world even thought it transcends the world: it is not the empirical situation but the natural fulfillment of it.

The certain standard which allows for universal knowledge and ethical norms is thus, in the teleological view, the essential nature of things which is never fully realized in empirical situations. To dismiss such an argument is tempting enough, in spite of the admitted deficiencies of relativism. Although science is less mechanically and more functionally oriented today than previously, natural law arguments still suffer from the liability of a conceptual framework long dismissed from most sciences of natural phenomena. This in

[19] John Wild, "Natural Law and Modern Ethical Theory," *Ethics*, LXIII (October, 1952), pp. 1–13.

itself does not make natural law either true or false, for if every theory does indeed rest on assumptions which cannot be proved (as is demonstrated with the presence of boundaries in all inquiry), then teleology is no more tenuously grounded than modern science.

But the utility of a theory cannot be entirely identified with the certainty of its premises. We would only fall into absurdities if we argued that the explanatory power of a teleological framework is superior, or equal to, that of contemporary scientific theory. In terms of understanding the processes of physical things a Newtonian or a post-Einstein approach would have more efficacy than an inquiry into final causes. This means that the classical doctrine of natural law, as described so far, must encounter the positivist objection that teleology does not adequately account for the way in which the world moves.

One way for natural law theorists to escape this difficulty is to divorce natural law from natural phenomena and confine it to the area of human behavior. Besides avoiding a direct confrontation with the positivist case built on modern science, this allows the distinction between two kinds of law: descriptive and prescriptive. Descriptive law formulates the regularities of phenomena, while prescriptive law denotes those rules requiring men to behave in certain ways. This distinction indicates that prescriptive law may be broken and still remain law in the sense of unfulfilled obligation, while it is senseless to say of descriptive law that it either can or cannot be broken. The reason that this latter observation is inappropriate is that if descriptive law does not coincide with phenomena it is simply reformulated to fit the phenomena.[20]

If natural law is confined to human obligation, then it may be totally unrealized (denoting as it does only what men ought to do), but is always partially unrealized. Thus, we must, if this position is to be defended, deny that human

[20] H.L.A. Hart, *The Concept of Law*. (Oxford: Clarendon Press, 1961), pp. 181–89.

norms always satisfy the natural demands of ethics and knowledge (even though they might usually do so). The fundamental claim of natural law taken in this way is that certain principles exist, awaiting discovery by human reason, with which man-made norms must conform if they are to be valid.[21] Notice that this can be viewed as a teleological notion, for the principles implied here can be seen as the natural end or goal of man not constructed or consciously intended by him. But the teleology of this natural law argument applies only to human beings, and not to the things of nature. Hence, the arguments of modern science are avoided.

LEO STRAUSS

The second position in natural law, which relies not on teleology but on the unchanging structure of the natural world, can be poignantly demonstrated in the natural right theory of Leo Strauss.[22] As a strong, indeed vehement, dissenter from the positivist influence in political science, Strauss also constructs his theory on an objective standard independent of both divine and human ordinance. But the question of change or natural development always remains marginal to Strauss' main considerations. It is the whole of *being* which constitutes the source of his natural standards. *Becoming*, or change, is marginal to his concern with unchanging standards.

Being, or nature, could function for Strauss as the unrealized purpose of man, much as it does for Aristotle. But we would misconstrue his argument to take his notion of natural things in terms of teleological development. In spite of his general affinity for both Plato and Aristotle, Strauss is much closer to the Platonic source of natural principles than he is

---

[21] *Ibid.*

[22] One of the clearer statements of Strauss' dissent is in his *What is Political Philosophy?* (Glencoe, Ill.: The Free Press, 1959).

to Aristotle's teleology. The important distinction for Strauss is that between nature and convention. It is to nature that Strauss looks for standards, and nature, for him, does not change.

A distinction between natural right and natural law need not be exhaustively pursued here. Certainly law often suggests a development, or pattern of movement, while the idea of right implies a just claim, or that which is due anyone from a just claim. We may then appropriately say that teleology is a form of natural law, and the Straussian-Platonic notion of objective principles is not. But both the developmental patterns of nature and objective principles are the basis for rights, at least in the sense that specific claims are to be viewed as just or unjust as they accord with the natural order of things.

The important thing about both natural law and natural right is the effect they have on the concept of duty. A duty is nothing more than the fulfillment of just claims, or that which one is bound to do by moral or legal obligation. If, as in the modern notion of natural right developed by Hobbes, the construction of rights is entirely within society, then the relationship between rights and duty is entirely reciprocal: no rights exist without duties, nor duties without rights. To fulfill a just claim is, in this case, to fulfill the rights of other people. But in the classic use of natural law and right, duty can be an obligation to an ideal order outside of society; and hence duties can exist which do not directly fulfill any other person's rights. Therefore the distinction between classic and modern right is to be found not only in the varying emphases on duty itself, but in the kinds of things to which obligation is directed.

For Strauss, the forms defining obligation are found in that part of the world which is unaffected by convention (the artifice of human beings). If, that is, one could place in abeyance the whole of human constructions, then the world as given would be the natural order yielding epistemic and ethical standards. More than just the faint presence of phenomenology is here. In Husserl's thought, for example, one finds an attempt to reduce the phenomena of experience to their essential natures. The model used by Husserl is that of a polarized consciousness housing both subject and object. Thought is taken as intentional, or thought as always *of* something. In the commonsense world, we encounter the objects of thought from a perspective consisting of learned expectations. Suspending this perspective allows us to view in an originary sense that which constitutes our existence.

So, too, does Strauss want to confront that basic nature unaffected by human distortion. Understandably, the two positions he considers most antagonistic to this thesis are History and the argument that there is a distinction between facts and values. By History Strauss seems to mean historicism, or that approach claiming that all principles are mutable because they are products of historical conditions. Both these positions comprise the main attack on natural right and are characteristic of modern social science, in Strauss's opinion, and he unleashes most of his own antagonism precisely at these closely related themes. The attack is certainly stimulating, but (as we shall see) only partially effective.

The more shopworn arguments against historicism have been dealt with earlier, and so we need mention only in passing the classic criticism of relativism subjecting the historicist argument to its own claims. But there are several twists Strauss manages to get into his critique, which finally allow him to use the main observations of historicism to support the natural rights argument. This move has its footing in the basic claim of the historicist argument: that the existence of a multitude of beliefs all defining right or justice in conflicting fashion is clear evidence that no universal right exists. Strauss correctly dismisses the necessity of consensus for the existence of natural right, but then claims that the very existence of such pluralism is the basis for the discovery of natural right.

Several ideas are implied here. First, Strauss holds that the very fact that justice is defined, regardless of how the specific interpretations of the notion differ, suggests that a universal need exists for one principle. That is, fragments seem to demand the imposition of the whole. Second, Strauss feels that even antithetical interpretations of justice share a common feature. They all point to the same thing, however imperfectly. Finally, the method that Strauss defends for discovering justice, the Socratic dialectic, must begin with conflicting opinions. All of these ideas are central to the method of classical philosophy.

The universal principle referred to here (as indicated earlier) derives from being itself; and we can, according to Strauss, secure knowledge of the whole of being. This is, in fact, the fundamental task of philosophy for Strauss: replacing opinions about the whole with knowledge of the whole. This means that the whole of being is identical with the whole as object of human intelligence, for knowledge of the whole presupposes that being in its entirety can be apprehended by the knowing subject. It does not overwhelm him. Even more: that being, since it is the object of inquiry, is identical with the intelligible; and the whole of being is coincidental with full intelligence. The entirety of being is always the same. To be is always to be. There is, in this view, no other way that it is sensible to speak of being except in terms of constancy. Otherwise a thing is not; it is only becoming. Historicism denies this notion of entirety, holding that existence is incomplete, and not capable of fulfillment. It is forever changing and not intelligible except partially.

The knowledge of being referred to in this version of natural rights theory is personal. Philosophizing means "to ascend from public dogma to essentially private knowledge.[23] This makes the acceptance of universal principles, as Strauss is quick to point out, a revolutionary undertaking, at least in the sense that it involves judging the established order by a rational or natural norm. The actual will always fall short of the ideal. If not, the universal would not be an ideal. Such a discrepancy can lead to difficulty if it is pointed out often enough. This has not been a totally unknown fact since Socrates abruptly discovered it.

Historicists generally reject universals, and thus probably have less trouble with those who have no time to consider the matter either way. But historicism and skepticism are not synonymous as used here. For the skeptic, all assertions are uncertain and arbitrary. This amounts to a kind of self-consistent paradox, since, again, this claim must also be regarded in the same way. Historicism, on the other hand, tries to define definitively the limits of human knowledge within which genuine knowledge is possible. These limits are determined by the local and the temporal, which as specifics are of higher value to historicists than the universal. The claims even of universality can be explained in historicism as products of cultural conditions, so the particular historical setting is the real source of knowledge; and the boundaries set by cultural conditions are those limits defining the scope of knowledge. Genuineness is possible within the framework so circumscribed.

There is an easy response to this line of argument, but Strauss adopts it with difficulty. Defining limits presupposes going beyond these limits in the sense of implying an area outside of what is circumscribed. To draw limits, after all, is to define a specific part or boundary, which unavoidably suggests something not included, however hazy this area of exclusion might be. This was pointed out in the discussion of Ayer's thesis. Strauss moves in this direction, but the only

[23] Leo Strauss, *Natural Right and History* (Chicago: University of Chicago Press, 1953), p. 12.

criticism he can make is that historicism is inconsistent: it needs an absolute moment in history when the essential limitation of all thought is apprehended, and this moment is necessarily beyond local and temporal boundaries. This is correct, though tendentious. What Strauss is ignoring is a basic similarity between historicism and the natural rights position growing out of a common rigidity of style. Absolute moments can hardly be criticized by natural rights theorists. No matter at the moment. Strauss confines this part of his criticism to one special and important point, which is that we cannot explain the ideas of philosophers, especially earlier thinkers, in terms of social forces because the specific limitations of human thought are essentially unknowable.

One final vulnerability of the historicist position seduces Strauss, as it does every critic. This is the thesis that all knowledge presupposes a frame of reference within which knowing takes place; and this comprehensive view cannot be validated by reasoning, since it is the basis of all reasoning. Accordingly, one must choose (or have imposed upon him) a comprehensive view without any rational guidance. It is a familiar position, and the argument against it has been mentioned too many times up to now to need elaboration, which is that the choice of such a viewpoint entails some stable principle or all knowledge is so hopelessly capricious that it is a contradiction in terms. Strauss dutifully makes these points. But the importance of his writings does not come from such prosaic arguments, for he is anxious to provide those very universals needed to make sense of every value judgment.

THE COMMON DIFFICULTY

The problem with Strauss's criticism of historicism, however, is precisely the universals to which it is tied. The deficiencies indicated so far in the historicist thesis are two. First, the charge of inconsistency has been made. By claim-

ing the historical contingency of all knowledge, the truth of
the historicist position has been accepted as independent of
circumstances. Second, we have the Kierkegaardian criticism
of Hegel. To establish the truth of the historicist thesis,
setting aside for the moment the internal problem of contradiction, would entail surveying the whole historical process.
This in turn presupposes an observer outside of history,
which is (as Kierkegaard saw) both impossible and absurd.

All of this is recognized by Strauss. But he encounters a
special kind of dilemma in adopting the Kierkegaardian
critique which would not hold for an open-ended position,
and that is that he cannot deny transcendence without under-
mining his own theory. Thus the historicist thesis can only
be self-contradictory to Strauss; and, by a curious twist of
style, both the radical historicist position and the natural
rights argument are vulnerable to the same critique: that
one cannot grasp a truth beyond circumstances without realizing an experience which is basically impossible, which is
going beyond the situation as given.

Consider once more what Strauss is claiming. The whole of
being is to be seen as object. This means that the subject, in
the moment of apprehending the whole, cannot properly be
a part of the whole. What Strauss means by the whole, after
all, is "all things," which is, in his own words, God, the
world, and man. This does not mean all contingencies, but
all things that participate in being. More specifically, the
whole as object of knowledge is the nature of all things,
or their essential features. But what is to become of the perceiving subject? The answer is unavoidable. In the confrontation with being he must transcend being. He must strip
himself of his place within the whole. For Kierkegaard, in
other words, both historicism and the philosophy of Strauss
would share a common liability.

What is even more to the point is the direction in which
transcendence takes us. When Kierkegaard says that a viewing of the whole is impossible, he means that such a sugges-

tion is contrary to ordinary modes of thought and expression. We seem to be involved in a contradiction at best, and a physical absurdity at worst. But the crucial issue here for Strauss is that in coming to understand the objective norm one gets beyond ordinary modes of thought and expression. It is a familiar story with a familiar answer. Like the Platonic Good, Strauss's standard is fugitive to commonsense criticism. But in escaping the absurd, both incur the burden of mysticism.

THEORIES AND PARADIGMS

The conclusion to be drawn from this discussion is an obvious one: the adoption of one philosophical framework or another always brings with it the peculiar liabilities and advantages of the framework chosen. Positivism comes encumbered with the problem of error, and hence relativism. On the other hand, a positivist approach maximizes lucidity. Metaphysics gets away from the relativist dilemma, but only by moving away from overt communication. The twin liabilities of relativism and opaqueness do not exhaust the characteristics of these two radically disparate approaches to knowledge, but each set of assumptions within these frameworks leads inexorably to one or the other of these difficulties.

Perhaps that is the point to remember. Conclusions follow from premises, and in accepting assumptions one must be prepared to accept the limiting frameworks which come out of them. The prior problem here is that the premises of a theoretical framework are not amenable to proof. We have seen that any philosophical claim rests on givens which must be accepted as a basis for getting on with the business of inquiry. Somewhere along the line, that is, the question of *why* one accepts something must be answered with a simple affirmation which cannot be proved by the theoretical system accepted.

What has emerged at this point in the discussion is a re-affirmation of theory as an instrument to solve problems, and not a description of reality. To ask of a positivist or a meta-physical approach whether it is truer than its opponent is, in the instrumental view, wholly inappropriate. What we must do is inquire about the range of events an approach embraces, the adequacy of its explanatory constructs, and the intellectual elegance of its concepts. This is another way of saying that theoretical frameworks do not more or less reflect the real world, but perform as devices to find one's way about the world; and whether one affirms one or another framework depends on its utility in doing what one sets out to do.

The crucial question is on what basis one sets out to do one thing instead of another. This brings us back to the observation made at the beginning of this section, which is that whether one infers a little or a lot from the world is finally the result of a commitment which eludes substantiation. This does not mean that choice is always blind, for we have demonstrated that strengths and liabilities are perceptible features of even the most radically antagonistic philosophical styles. But at the primordial level choice is at least unclear, for even the categorization of strengths and weaknesses is closely tied to one's *Weltanschauung*, and hence is prior to discourse itself. Because of this, we often speak of philosophical styles as paradigms, meaning they include one's world view as well as the overt theoretical scheme which is embraced.

One thing that is common to both positivism and metaphysics, however, is the point at which they begin: experience itself. The method common to classical philosophers and modern natural right theorists is the dialectic. This means (as Strauss points out) the art of conversation or friendly dispute. Hence dialectics starts with commonsense opinions, and by resolving the contradictions in common language the theorist ascends to the consistent or total view of truth. Positivism also begins with common language, but does not go beyond discourse to truths independent of mundane communication. No philosopher can totally ignore experience. The differences between theorists emerge in the kinds of conclusions one draws in coming to terms with the world.

On the other hand, these conclusions can differ considerably. Sometimes the only similarity between theoretical frameworks is their common point of departure. We need not be surprised, therefore, that individuals with different paradigms often talk past each other. To communicate intelligibly entails some common ground, and the absence of communication between some of the contrasting viewpoints to be discussed later will indicate how different are the premises and conclusions constructed from the human experience. We can, however, draw more profit for ourselves from the discussions if we bear in mind the presence of some of the differing assumptions delineated up to now.

CHAPTER III

Function and Causality
in the Social Sciences

ORIGINS

Theories exhibit various patterns of explanation. These are visible characteristics, and may be investigated as features which are more overt than the philosophical frameworks we have encountered up to now. No explanatory pattern is logically deducible from assumptions which are more tacit, but the adequacy of an explanation is determined by our predispositions toward the legitimate boundaries explanations may take. Causality in a metaphysical framework is self-evident proof of God's existence.[1] A positivist treatment of the same explanatory pattern stays within the limits of sense experience.

[1] This proof goes back at least to Aquinas.

Some patterns of explanation are more common than others. A linguistic explanation simply defines a word, or demonstrates its implications. Definition may be either nominal, stipulative, empirical, or analytic.[2] Indicating why a thing is true or false constitutes another kind of explanation. Also, we may explain how something came to be as it is, which is a causal explanation.[3] The most generally used form of scientific explanation is subsuming an event under an empirical regularity.[4] For adequacy this entails a causal sequence also, although strictly speaking it may not. That is, in one sense we have explained why crow X is black with the answer that all crows are black. But the questioner may understandably be impatient with such an answer, for a satisfactory response probably would have to include a causal explanation of why all crows are black.

One of the basic explanatory modes in the social sciences is functional analysis. Analogically this approach may have its genesis in Darwinian biology, although the deeper intellectual roots can be traced back to classical teleology. The basic thesis in evolution is that an organism interacts with external stimuli in a way that engenders adaptation between the organism and the environment. The modern social categories of input-output and feedback are more than faintly familiar. From teleology comes the notion of goal-orientation. These dual origins have resulted in the attribution of both metaphysical and positivist characteristics to functional analysis.

Such basic parallels cannot be overdrawn, however, for like most generic developments the similarity between theory and source is fundamentally tenuous. The evolutionary

[2] Carl Hempel, *Problems of Concept Formation in Empirical Science* (Chicago: University of Chicago Press, 1952), pp. 1–20.

[3] Arnold Brecht, *Political Theory* (Princeton, N.J.: Princeton University Press, 1959), pp. 73–74.

[4] Ernest Nagel, *The Structure of Science* (New York: Harcourt, Brace & World, 1961), pp. 117–52.

framework embraces an entirely neutral process, or one where adaptation is not a conscious enterprise. The environment does not choose (as we think of the term choice) the best plants and animals to live, and plants and animals certainly do not consciously select one advantageous set of characteristics or another. Certain features of life win out because they have made for the survival of a greater proportion of the organisms possessing these features. Probabilities, not desires, run evolution. In social systems, on the other hand, human beings consciously manipulate their settings.

We should not, however, leap quickly to the conclusion that functionalism can be tied only to purposive behavior. Quite the contrary will be demonstrated. The ends which men construct are by no means always functional for their social systems, nor are all functions synonymous with human goals of some sort. What is more to the point is that a degree of functional analysis extends over both physiological and social explanations, although social theorists must always take into account in *some* fashion the conscious intentions of human beings (which biologists do not have to do). This is true even though purpose may be seen as probabilistic, and desire as a random occurrence.

We also should not confuse an explanation of goal-oriented behavior with teleology. The Aristotelian version of development, as we have seen, assumes a final goal which directs prior conditions. This is not modern causality in reverse, for the asymmetrical relationship of antecedent to result is only one small part of the Aristotelian framework. What a teleological explanation does is collapse the time dimension of empirical causality in the notion of potentiality. Strictly speaking the final goal is a future state, but as the essence of a thing it exists potentially in the thing. Hence what a thing fundamentally *is* also denotes what it is to become. But functionalism employs neither future states nor potential existence. Actors in a social system may have purposes, but these goals are taken as factual states existing in the present and not as future units exerting an effect on the present.

Distinct as functional analysis may be from its intellectual beginnings, though, its distinctiveness as an explanatory approach may still be questioned. To be sure, the plethora of work purporting to be functional analysis assumes that the method is a different kind of enterprise from straightforward scientific explanation. Nevertheless, an argument can be constructed that functional analysis is nothing more than a series of if–then propositions of the sort, "if function X, then functioning system Y"; and hence functional analysis is nothing more or less than a version of causal explanation.[5] Accordingly, the initial task in any discussion of functionalism is determining whether or not it is a separate mode of inquiry.

HUMAN GOALS

One basis for distinguishing functional analysis from other explanatory approaches may be rejected immediately, as we have already suggested. This is the notion that social phenomena are distinct from all other kinds of phenomena by virtue of the fact that human behavior is purposive; and that this distinctive feature of social data is inextricably linked to functional analysis. To the first part of this notion one can only give assent. Social behavior is unquestionably goal-oriented. But the tight involvement of functionalism with this characteristic is erroneous. The questions suggested by this involvement are whether purposes can only be ex-

[5] Both Ernest Nagel, a philosopher of science, and Kingsley Davis, a sociologist, argue that functionalism is simply standard scientific inquiry. See Nagel's "Problems of Concept and Theory Formation in the Social Sciences," *Science, Language and Human Rights* (American Philosophical Association, Eastern Division, Philadelphia: University of Pennsylvania Press, 1952, Vol. I), pp. 43–64. Davis puts forth his argument in "The Myth of Functional Analysis," *American Sociological Review* (1959), pp. 757–72.

plained functionally, and also whether functional explanation is confined only to purposive behavior. The answer to both these questions is no.

To explain an event functionally means that the event is seen in terms of its relationship to an ongoing system. What this distinctive feature does *not* mean is almost as important as what it does mean. Most importantly, no assumption is made that the event explained is in a positive relationship with the system enclosing it, either in the sense that all system units are integrated or that units exist which are indispensable to the maintenance of the system.[6] Such qualifications are by now classic. On the other hand, we must not overlook the fact that an event explained functionally must always be conceptualized from the perspective of an enclosing system, for functions are relational concepts. Hence, whatever the special nature of an event's consequences for a system—whether it is functional in a positive sense, disfunctional, or neutral—the event must be viewed in terms of its relationship to a whole other than itself if it is to be explained functionally.

On this account of functional and general scientific inquiry, we have no reason to believe, first, that purposes can only be explained functionally. A purpose, as indicated earlier, is a factual state, and thus expressible in the following form: "It is a fact now to be taken into account that actor X possesses goal Y." This kind of a variable may be viewed as an instance of an empirical regularity, or as an event to be conceptualized in terms of a system. One form of inquiry or another may be more efficacious in explaining social events, but the efficacy will derive from the view of society either as a system, or as a collection of discrete events. We may even go so far as to say that goal-oriented behavior is more completely explained in a system framework, but this is a separate question whose answers still would not

[6] Robert Merton, *Social Theory and Social Structure* (Glencoe: The Free Press, 1964), pp. 25–37.

void the conclusion that purposes may be subsumed, as facts, under empirical regularities.

To the second question, whether functionalism can explain only purposive behavior and no other, the conclusion is also negative. This is evident when one realizes that a function means an objective consequent, or system event constructed by the analyst and not by the actor. No concept suffers from more definitional ambiguity than function, but one common feature which secures modern agreement is precisely that functions are not necessarily coincidental with the intentions of actors.[7] This means that functional analysis is not, even in application to human behavior, inextricably tied to purposes. Functionalism focuses on purposes only insofar as they relate to the social system; and the thought that functional analysis only treats human goals results from erroneously collapsing goals and functional events.

This rejection of the argument based on purpose unavoidably expands functional analysis to phenomena other than human. What is now crucial to functionalism is the notion of *system*, which may be a characteristic of both social and natural phenomena. Again, this does not deny the distinctiveness of social phenomena, which presents the analyst with additional (and perhaps more complex) variables to take into account. The point is that a *functional* explanation of these variables is conducted in a manner which is similar to functional explanations of nonhuman behavior, even given the fact that purposes may have to be introduced as additional considerations into any treatment of human systems.

Abandoning the purposive argument may be rationalized on two grounds. First, we may claim (as we have done here) that functionalists do not in the literature use the concept in a way that ties them to purposive variables. This is certainly true, although not definitive. The literature, it may be said, is only as valid as its contemporary critics make it out to be.

[7] *Ibid.*, pp. 50–54.

The second reason is more satisfying: to link functional analysis wholly to purposive phenomena is to create problems which can be easily avoided in a system conceptualization of functionalism, and without loss of advantage. This rationale is also developed in the literature, with great persuasiveness, and we will do this here as well.

Accordingly, the salient question is whether functional analysis as a way of looking at *both* social and physical data in a system is a separate mode of inquiry. Or, put more specifically, we must determine if functionalism is anything other than the conditional causality of if–then propositions linking one event to another.

Causality

To answer this question we must get into the meaning of causal explanation. The classic dilemma of causality broached by Hume remains with us. Briefly, it is that from the conjunction of two empirical events A and B one cannot establish that they are causally related. This impossibility emerges from the requirements contained in the idea of causality which cannot be fulfilled empirically. Two of these are of particular significance. One is the notion of forcing, or A bringing into being B. No amount of observation can verify this requirement, for all that can be observed is the correlation of A and B. The other requirement is that of continuance. If A occurs at any time, then we would expect without fail the occurrence of B if the relationship is causal. But the basic fact that the future is open-ended, or indeterminate by definition, prevents empirical validation of this requirement.

A word of qualification is needed here. The concept of a causal relationship must not be constructed too severely. No more than a sufficient condition is needed for causality, which means that whenever the independent variable A occurs, then the dependent variable must occur. To impose necessity on the relationship is too rigorous a requirement, for this would mean that B could never occur without A. That this is unrealistic for the ordinary expectations of a causal relationship can be demonstrated easily enough with an example. We might say that heart attacks of a certain degree of severity (A) cause death (B), and that the relationship is a sufficient one in that whenever A, then B. But we would not want to claim necessity, for certainly death could occur on a number of grounds other than heart attacks of the sort constituting the independent variable.

The dissent from the construction of causality around only sufficient conditions is a familiar one. It is this: if B occurs when A is not present, then one has no assurance that A truly is the causal variable. We can easily imagine a situation where A is always accompanied by an unknown variable C, which in actuality is the causal agent. When B occurs without A, then C (within this formulation) would still be present as an unknown factor in the variables which are recognized (X, Y, Z). Hence C, not A, is the real causal variable in the relationship. In the example used, death would be caused not by the heart attacks, but by a third factor, C, which is always antecedent to death even though precipitating or precipitated by a number of different conditions (heart attacks being one of them).

The third factor, C, may occur prior to A, simultaneously with A, or intervening between A and B. In every case, if it is in a necessary relationship to B, it makes all other sufficient relationships between the dependent variable and stipulated causal agents spurious. Leaving aside for the moment the obvious empirical problem of ever obtaining a necessary relationship, the key point in this argument is that the variable C is unknown; for if it were known, then of course no other relationship except $C \rightarrow A$ would be postulated. What the proponents of this version of causality suggest is that if causality were defined in terms of both sufficient and necessary conditions, then the possibility of such a covert relationship would be voided.

The conclusion of this argument is true. On the other hand, conceptualizing causality to include necessary conditions produces more problems than it solves. The obvious difficulty of including within the concept many ordinary instances of causal relationships has already been mentioned. In terms of the previous example, one could not say that heart attacks of a given severity cause death, but only that this kind of heart attack precipitates another set of conditions which do in fact cause death, say the cutting off of oxygen to the brain. Relying on this condition, which intervenes between the heart attack and death, would fulfill the necessary relationship between causal agent and effect; for we could then say that death would never occur unless oxygen is cut off from the brain. With this as the real cause of death, then all other seeming causes would be viewed as causative only of the cessation of oxygen. Or, that is, as sufficient but not necessary conditions.

But this addition of necessity is odd to the point of absurdity. If pursued, then we have no basis for separating independent and dependent variables within the causal sequence. Could death be distinguished from the cessation of oxygen to the brain? Part of this problem is operationalizing one's concepts to the point where death would be defined as a specific set of conditions, and any other conditions related to it would be viewed as separate variables. In this sense the dependent variable (death) *could* be operationalized as a set of physiological conditions subsequent to the cessation of oxygen to the brain. This operationalism in turn may vary from one empirical design to another.

But the question of distinctions still may be asked about the operational design if it relies on both a necessary and sufficient relationship between the two variables. To operationalize a concept means to state it in a way that it can be empirically verified, or measured. If the causal sequence is the fulfillment of both necessary and sufficient conditions, however, then no factual base is available in this conceptualization to substantiate the operational distinction. If whenever A, then B, and, also, whenever B, then A, then this means A and B always occur together. Factually, that is, they are one event, for not even in principle can they be separated in the formulation as it stands. The discontinuance of oxygen to the brain is part of the factual event known as death.

Of course, if we get away from the unhappy example used up to now, a separation between causal events (related on both sufficient and necessary grounds) could be attempted on the basis of location within a space-time matrix. That is, one could say that necessary and sufficient relationships could occur between variables differing in where they occur and when they occur. But, if one inspects this assertion at all closely, peculiar difficulties still arise. Any factual event, by definition, occupies a spatial and temporal category. To say of a necessary and sufficient relationship that it constitutes two events, or variables, entails more than that the beginning and the end of the event occupy different places on a space-time continuum, for this also is true of a single event. One must ordinarily say that the antecedent variable in such a relationship is separated from the dependent variable by intervening factors.

The difficulty with this formulation is that it often is still inadequate, and in any case makes the establishment of causality dependent on factors which are additional to the primary causal relationship. This means that causality cannot be demonstrated simply on the basis of necessary and sufficient conditions, which are in themselves never enough to establish a separation between independent and dependent variables, but that a proof is also needed which reveals the occurrence of events which are temporally and spatially between A and B. Again, this is not an impossible task, but it hardly demonstrates separate variables in all cases.

One brief example will demonstrate why this is so. The survey design of *The American Voter* correlates attitudinal states with voting behavior.[8] To infer a causal relationship between attitudes and behavior on the basis of necessary and sufficient conditions is an absurdity. If we say that a man voted for Eisenhower, as the authors claim, because he likes him, this analysis can only be justified on the grounds of a separation between liking and voting. That is, only as attitude and behavior are *not* inextricably linked can we assume that they are separate variables and that we have not constructed a tautology in place of an explanation. Factors intervening between these two variables have (obviously) no bearing on this relationship. What is needed, curiously enough, are instances when the two are not correlated.

Other difficulties with a closed (necessary and sufficient) causality bear mentioning. Postulating sufficient conditions as a ground for causality is consistent with the general notion of empirical claims, which are probable but never certain; for sufficient conditions never exhaust the class of antecedent variables taken as causal for the dependent variable. To say of A that it is sufficient for the occurrence of B leaves open the possibility that B will occur as the result of variables which are *not* A. But the introduction of necessary conditions to the sufficient relationship closes the claim, for necessary conditions may be taken as the exhaustive or completed class of sufficient conditions. If we knew all the sufficient conditions, then this would be coincidental with the necessary conditions. This establishment of a closed class makes the construction of causality analytic, and hence without general empirical referents.

We should not be surprised that small group studies in the social sciences and mathematical models in the physical sciences allow for the construction of causal sequences constituted by necessary and sufficient relationships. It is precisely the fact that they are artificial situations which makes

[8] Angus Campbell *et al.*, *The American Voter* (New York: John Wiley & Sons, 1960), pp. 64–88.

possible the development of an analytic version of causality. To close out a class of factual items, after all, entails parameters for one's universe, which in this case would be the establishment of a finite number of independent variables. Otherwise one could not say that X class exhausts *all* possible instances of causal agents. But a closed system of this sort is not a truth of the empirical world, which is (as we have noted) open-ended by definition in terms of future occurrences. Hence if we are to make causal inferences about the factual world outside experimental designs, we must operate with a causality grounded only on sufficient conditions.

We should not conclude from this discussion that causality must apply only to sequences or continuing events. Causality can be conceptualized in terms of a single event never repeated, as when I take an object and release it. Even if taken as a unique event, we may correctly infer that my releasing the object caused it to drop to the earth. The telling feature here is that we may conceptually universalize the event to say that whenever objects are released under certain conditions this causes them to drop to the earth, which gives the relationship the sufficient form of "if A, then B." This conceptual universality demonstrates still another point, which is that events can be explained scientifically at different levels of generality. In this case, I may explain the object dropping to earth *because* I released it, or *because* it is an instance of gravitational theory. The first type of explanation is simple causality, while the second is subsumption under a general law (which, as we have seen, usually includes causality for reasons of adequacy).

Causality and Correlation

None of this deals with the Humean dilemma. This should not be so surprising, for to meet Hume's objection in the way that it is framed is impossible. Factual assertions are probable, while causality must be certain. One dimension to this problem can be dealt with, as we have demonstrated, by relaxing the *necessary* feature of a causal relationship. This allows dependent variables to have an indeterminate class of causal agents, which is consistent with the notion of contingency in empirical propositions. But the framing even of *sufficient* conditions is contrary to factual occurrences, for we simply cannot say that A will always cause B without a glimpse into the entire range of future events. Event A may occur at some time without B, and thus we have a correlation between A and B but not a causal relationship.

Hume's objection can, however, be avoided in actual research. This may be done by taking empirical theories not as true–false representations of phenomena, but as instruments to order experience.[9] In this way, no causality need obtain between empirical events, for the properties and relationships of events can be considered part of the theoretical framework instead of features of the factual universe. Hence while causality still is not verifiable *in* the world, it may be ascribed to events for purposes of accomplishing certain tasks in analysis. The question of whether causality really holds can in this fashion be set aside as inappropriate for scientific research.

Most of what goes on in social science research is based (implicitly or explicitly) on such a move. Strictly speaking, causality is a feature only of the research design, although inferences about causality in events can be made on the basis of correlation. In such cases one is drawing conclusions about the possibility of actual causality, although the factual evidence to confirm such a relationship always remains fugitive to the analyst. This does not deny the establishment of a probability that causality between events does in fact hold. In general the degree of correlation between variables func-

[9] See the arguments presented in Chapter I. Also, refer to Nagel, *The Structure of Science, op. cit.*, pp. 129–40.

tions as a confidence index for causality inferences. From this one may act *as if* causality obtains, although we must keep in mind that an establishment of factual causality is impossible.

Even the establishment of authentic correlation entails more than simple mathematical correspondence. If sunspots were perfectly correlated with business cycles, we still would not want to make an inference of causality between the two events. Here is where the notion of *forcing* comes into prominence. To postulate a causal relationship we need a reason (independent of correlation) to think that the antecedent variable is having an effect on the dependent variable. This reason is often based on our general conception of how things work in the universe, but a more systematic rationale emerges from the explanatory scheme itself: certain causal variables are excluded by fiat from possible classes of independent variables because they are not contiguous with the dependent variable in any apparent manner.

Once contiguity and mathematical correspondence are established, one must determine whether the correlation obtained between two variables occurring in sequence is due to the antecedent variable used in the correlation, or to some third variable affecting the dependent variable. For example, one may secure a correlation between the type of college an individual attends and the salary he earns after graduation. The conclusion then may be drawn that certain colleges, say those in the Ivy League, have a causal effect on later income. But the introduction of the family income of students as a third variable may demonstrate that individuals from wealthy families attend these better colleges, and in fact the level of family income is the definitive factor for salaries earned after graduation (due to the influence of the father, general contacts, etc.).

The techniques for establishing authentic correlation between variables (so that causality may be inferred) are numerous. Some of the earlier approaches can be found in

Herbert Hyman's *Survey Design*.[10] A newer set of techniques has been argued in Hubert Blalock's *Causal Inferences in Nonexperimental Research*.[11] To go over an adequate sample of these techniques would be a chapter in itself.[12] Only one point is necessary to our discussion here: aside from the obvious problems of quantifying the variables and securing the data, the crucial part of correlation is identifying the variables and conceptualizing them so that one is measuring the designated attribute and nothing else. Whatever the technique adopted, accuracy remains a product of the research scheme.

Functional Analysis

On the basis of the preceding discussion, a distinction between functionalism and a straightforward causal analysis can now be demonstrated. To do this, though, entails that we recognize what would constitute a case for the separation at issue. One way of viewing the distinctiveness of a mode of inquiry is in terms of its requirements for a satisfactory explanation. What kind of an answer, we may ask, will fulfill a request for a causal demonstration, and what answer will meet the requirements of functional analysis?

We have seen that the fundamental notion in functional analysis is that of seeing an event in terms of its relationship to a system. The idea of a system is fundamental because of the relational nature of the concept function. By relational we mean that a function has to function *for* something else; it cannot exist alone *as a function*. Further, when we

---

[10] Hyman, *Survey Design* (Glencoe, Ill.: The Free Press, 1955).

[11] Blalock, *Causal Inferences in Nonexperimental Research* (Chapel Hill: The University of North Carolina Press, 1964).

[12] For a good compendium of the more sophisticated techniques, see Hayward Alker's "Causal Inference and Political Analysis," soon to be published in Joseph Berud, ed., *Mathematical Application in Political Science* (Dallas: Southern Methodist University Press, forthcoming).

speak of social functions we also mean a class activity. One cannot say of an event, A, that it is functional for some other event, Y, unless the two events are related generally. This means that functions can only be kinds of events, and not simply specific units. A given act of voting can be seen as functional to a political system only as it is subsumed under the general class of activities conceptualized as voting.

In mathematics we speak of functions as mathematical quantities whose values depend upon the values of other quantities. In this sense, a functional relationship may be viewed as change $\rightarrow$ consequence between individual variables. But on this level a functional relationship *is* simple causality, and as such ignores the system relationship which obtains even in mathematics when quantities are varying interdependently. As used in social analysis, functional relationships separate from causality as they take into account the social framework formed by interacting social variables.

The meaning of a system is basic enough: it is a collectivity comprised of individual units interacting in a state of mutual dependence. Strictly speaking, two units can constitute the minimum dimensions of a system, but ordinarily we speak of systems as being composed of more numerous relationships. The important point for our discussion is that functional events *are* the units comprising a system; and so when we refer to units as functional or dysfunctional for a system, we must remember that we are not speaking of mutually exclusive variables in reference to units and systems. A functional unit is part of the definition of its system.

This overlap does not mean that a system's properties are totally exhausted by the individual characteristics of its units. As we shall see in a moment, system variables in social analysis cannot be reduced to the constituent parts of a system without loss of meaning for the system variables. But we must also understand that a function $\rightarrow$ system relationship does not indicate separate independent and dependent variables, for a system cannot be defined without reference to its units and the functional relationships of these units. Further, when we explain any specific event functionally, we place it in a system (or relational) framework; and this means we have defined the event only in terms of its system properties. The definitional overlap is reciprocal.

An example demonstrating this point might be helpful. If we explain the act of voting functionally, then we strip from this event all effects that are not relevant to the system in which it is functioning. Normally we take voting in terms of a political system, although a functional explanation may be predicated on any of a number of different systems. As a political act, however, voting is conceptualized in terms of its relationship to a political system which has as one of its properties the activity of voting. This conceptualization creates standards of relevance which allow for the dismissal of nonsystem effects of voting, such as the wear and tear on automobile tires which results from driving to the polls. Both unit (voting) and system (political phenomena) definitionally lean on each other.

Again, the system's properties cannot be equated with the simple aggregation of unit properties. In any unit–whole relationship the link between units and whole differs in accordance with the nature of the whole. In some instances parts can be added to get the whole, as three feet constitute a yard. In other cases addition is inappropriate, for the densities of parts cannot be added to get the density of a whole comprised of those parts. At times the order of the parts is crucial in defining a whole, as when notes arranged in a certain way go to make up a melody. In Gestalt theory, the whole conditions the total definitions of parts.[13]

The feature upon which the unit–whole relationship turns in each case is the kind of theoretical framework defining

[13] Ernest Nagel, "On the Statement 'The Whole is More than the Sum of its Parts'," in Paul Lazarsfeld and Morris Rosenberg, eds., *The Language of Social Research* (Glencoe, Ill.: The Free Press, 1957), pp. 519–32.

and explaining the phenomena under consideration. With the concept of density, the relationship is one thing; in harmonic theory still another; and so on.[14] This unit–group division is not (as the examples affirm) a metaphysical proposition, but an empirical claim amenable to verification. In systems theory treating social phenomena, the properties of the whole cannot be exhaustively derived from the characteristics of constituent units. When explaining the nature of groups, say, one is analyzing relationships which constitute what is distinctive about the group as a collectivity, and which are not reducible without loss of meaning to the characteristics of human beings belonging to the groups. We must emphasize that this is not the claim that a social collectivity exists independently of its members (for no social system could exist without human beings), but only that taken as a system it is *different* than the private features of its units.

This claim for system variables can be demonstrated in hundreds of ways. When we study legislative behavior, the activity of a legislative body can never be adequately explained by the personal characteristics of its members. One must also take into account the role structure of the legislature, or those variables which are part of the collectivity. Pressure to conform to a modal pattern of behavior in a labor union cannot be derived from individual members, but from the members interacting in a way that results in a group effect. These examples can be multiplied endlessly. They all demonstrate one point: a social system at any level cannot be seen as equivalent to a collection of individual units, for a system possesses its own distinctive features.

What is suggested by this view of a system is the operation of feedback. A functional unit is defined in terms of its system relationship, and these unit-characteristics comprise the system in question. But the existence of a system en-

[14] *Ibid.*

genders system variables which have an effect on the units making up the social aggregate.

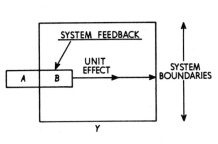

AB = functional unit
   (Ex.: voting)

Y = political system

A = nonsystem effects
   (Ex.: wearing out of tires on the way to the polls)

B = system effects
   (Ex.: election of a liberal rather than a conservative candidate)

Further, since the relationship of unit to system is a continuing one, we would expect even the conceptualizations of unit effects and system boundaries to be a variable of these exchanges. It is even possible to visualize a political system where tire attrition *is* a unit effect on the system.

From this brief delineation, the characteristics distinctive of functionalism should be evident. They may be stated briefly. First, a functional explanation always focuses on the relationship of events to some system. Second, a functional relationship is persistent activity, or an ongoing system. Third, the variables in functionalism are not mutually exclusive, but in fact overlap in definition. Fourth, functional activity is always in part reciprical. All of these features may be taken as necessary characteristics of any functional explanation in social analysis.

The differences between a functional and causal explanation can now be quickly made. To explain an event causally entails an establishment of precedence. Variable A cannot cause B unless A is antecedent to B. In functional analysis, however, both event and system exist at the same time.

Second, causality suggests forcing, or A bringing into being or changing B. The vector analogies of classical physics come to mind: the occurrence of A, or a change in A, results directly (after some time lapse, no matter how small) in the occurrence of B, or a change in B. No similar motif conditions functionalism, for functional states may vary concurrently with no apparent direction of force.

Further, causal explanation necessitates separate independent and dependent variables. If A causes B, then A is *not* B. But, as we have seen, a functional unit is part of its system. Finally, a causal relationship is asymmetrical. If we say that A causes B, this entails that B does not cause A. Causality is in this way uni-directional, or from one moment in time to the next. In functional analysis, on the other hand, the concept of feedback is an essential one. Not only does function A have consequences for system Y, but Y in turn conditions A.

$$\text{Causality} = A \rightarrow B$$

Functional Analysis =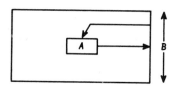

The objection to all of this might go as follows: All that a functional explanation does is causally link certain events to system states. To say that events are viewed from the framework of a system is nothing more than to say that multiple causality is operative, for the relationships between functional units and a system can be reduced to a series of causal events over time. To speak of functional consequences in the first place presupposes antecedent variables, as well as a change–effect relationship. Even the notion of feedback is causal, denoting that the system event has assumed the status of independent variable and is causing changes in the functional unit.

With this perspective, the dissent may continue, we can

say with perfect correctness that voting is causing certain system states, and these system states are having a causal effect on the activity of voting. Tire attrition may be excluded as well from this particular causal relationship, even though it may be explained causally in another context. Finally, to exclude causality in persisting systems is to ignore what persistence means, which is in this case that causal acts are being repeated over time. This means that any given event may be taken as a starting point for a causal analysis with no problem at all for the analysis.

The difficulty with this objection is that it begs the question. No one need deny that functional explanation can be broken down into a myriad of causal sequences any more than one would have to deny that subsumption of an event under an empirical regularity can be reduced to numerous causal events. The real question is what loss of meaning and efficiency results from doing so; and, even more importantly, whether or not we have a distinctive mode of inquiry even though this mode of inquiry can be broken down into constituent parts which, on the basis of the inquiry's purpose, constitute a different approach altogether.

The earlier recognition that an inquiry can be defined on the basis of its requirements for an adequate explanation demonstrates how these questions can be answered. When we ask for a functional analysis of social events, we are asking for considerably more than a causal explanation. What is required is a conceptualization of phenomena in terms of the features of functionalism which we have discussed. These features are not an entailment of causal analysis. So at the very least functional explanations are distinctive in this respect: that while causal relations may be a part of functional analysis, functional relations are not features of all causal explanations.

This disparity in explanatory requirements indicates the special nature of causality which places it within all explanatory schemes, yet keeps it distinct in equivalence from many. When we explain an event as an instance of Newton's laws of gravitation, it would be inappropriate to say that those laws *cause* events to fall. Yet, as we saw earlier, causal relations constitute the empirical process described by Newton's laws in the sense that gravity operates as an independent variable and the falling object as a dependent variable. But it would be erroneous to think that Newton's theory can be reduced to a series of causal relations without loss of meaning or distinctiveness.

The same kind of relationship holds between causality and functional theory. With functionalism we are proceeding at a different level of generality with different purposes. To be sure, causality is suggested by functional analysis in the form of "if function A, then system state B." But to leave the analysis there and claim equivalence is to miss the distinctive kinds of things which functionalism does. The universality of causality in explanatory schemes derives from the fact that explanation focuses on things happening to one another over time. This is no less true in functional relations, where unit–system processes can be thought of as numerous sequences of causal relations.

But this fact does not make functional analysis coincidental with causal analysis. In functional explanations we are treating things which happen to one another in a special way, and this goes considerably beyond simple causality. The separation of modes of inquiry finally turns on the way in which we conceptualize and relate phenomena. Events and relations between events are not given to us in a self-evident manner. What is distinctive about functional analysis is that it takes events in terms of system relationships, which causality need not do, and hence it cannot be transformed into causal analysis without a change in meaning or direction of inquiry.

To revert back to the example of voting: we may construct either a causal or a functional explanation of this event. A causal analysis would outline the sufficient antecedent factors if voting were conceptualized as a dependent variable, or the effects if voting were taken as an independent variable. As an independent variable, we might infer that the turnout in county A brought about the election of candidate Smith. A functional explanation, on the other hand, would entail a conceptualization of voting as a unit specifically related to an ongoing system which in turn conditions the act of voting. Negro voting, we may say, is a demand upon the political system which alters the system to include even more Negroes in the system's definition of the franchise.

An earlier point must be brought up again. This elaboration of functional analysis is in part empirical. By this is meant that it is a description of the way in which functional analysis is conducted in the literature. But no field is totally consistent, and so the explanation of functionalism given here is also stipulative. It is posed, that is, as the correct way to view functional analysis. The grounds for this assertion are modest enough: if one does not define functionalism in terms of system requirements, then the approach is not separate from causal analysis and one is left with no distinctive mode of inquiry over which to argue. This proposition is the heart of the foregoing delineation.

Functionalism and Operational Requirements

As an independent approach, however, the problems of functional analysis are legion. Most are well known; some are not. The most immediate difficulties are those of drawing empirical inferences from the approach as an applied method. The use of deduction is impossible, for one cannot deduce the existence of a functional unit from the existence of a system unless one assumes that the unit is indispensable for the given condition of the system. Deductive movement from an existent unit to the state of a system must also be predicated on a necessary relationship.[15] Indispensability,

---

[15] Hempel, "The Logic of Functional Analysis," in Llewelyn Gross, ed., *Symposium on Sociological Theory* (New York: Harper & Row, 1959), pp. 271–302.

however, is one of the cardinal empirical mistakes of functional analysis.[16]

We cannot, that is, assume that voting is necessarily present in all political systems; or that voting is always related (when it is present) to certain system states. If we cannot, though, then it is impossible to deductively move from the observation that a political system exists to the conclusion that people vote. Nor, to turn the example around, can we deductively conclude that because people are voting there must be a political system (although this derivation is a more likely conclusion on the basis of factual evidence than the first). Of even more relevance than the second derivation is the impossibility of deducing conditions of the political system from the existence of voting. This deductive problem holds even when the cleavage between voting $\rightarrow$ existence of a political system is voided by positing voting as a sufficient condition in the definition of a political system.

Even probability inferences remain tenuous in functional analysis. To say with some degree of certainty that system states lead to certain functional units, or vice versa, entails a specification of functional alternatives; for probability is the number of instances of a unit in a given class, and unless the class can be determined no probability statement can be constructed. This means that the empirical question of what class of items constitutes functions for a given system state, and what system states are compatible with various functional units, must be answered before functional analysis can generate factual probabilities.[17]

What these difficulties suggest is that boundaries in the form of finite classes for variables must be established both at the function and system level in order for functionalism to be operational. The variables at the function level would represent the kinds of units to be considered as functional

---

[16] Merton, *Social Theory and Social Structure, op. cit.*, pp. 32–37.
[17] Hempel, *op. cit.*, "The Logic of Functional Analysis."

alternatives; at the system level they would indicate the range of system states. In this way the possibility would be open for empirical projections of the sort, "functional unit X exists; therefore the system state of which X is a member must be A, B, C, or D." Or, "System state A exists; therefore functional unit X, Y, or Z must be present." Since the classes are established, the equivalent probability inference would be, "Functional unit X exists; therefore it is M/N probable that the system state will be A." Or, "System state A exists; therefore it is M/N probable that function X will be present."

Finite classes of this sort, which must be established for ongoing systems, are tenuous impositions on phenomena. What has occurred in the past constitutes the grounds for class construction. If voting has been associated with specific system states based on known instances, then these system states comprise the finite class of probable associations. The association between a system state and a range of functional alternatives also must be derived from available history. Within each class the degree of association between a single function and a single system state can be established. Unfortunately, the future movement of events constantly alters not only the limits of the class, but also the measures of association between specific functions and specific system states. This is true no matter how exhaustive the data on past relationships. With a small number of cases, probability inferences are even more tenuous.

The problem of boundaries arises in still another connection. In physiology the external limits of a system are usually not problematic. There is no question, for example, about where a system like the human body begins and where it ends. In the social sciences this question is not so easily answered, for the accidents of geography are not so neatly congruent with conceptual categories: where, say, the United States social system begins and ends is a problem in itself. The boundaries of systems like the political and economic present even more complex difficulties, for they represent subsystems conceptually located within the notion of a social system. Hence, a problem which is logically prior to any other in functional analysis is specifying what phenomena are to count as instances of the system in question, for without the specific establishment of system boundaries functional explanation is impossible.

Boundaries: Social Systems

A system, as indicated earlier, is a set of interacting units in a state of mutual dependence. Perhaps the most misused concept associated with mutual dependence is that of equilibrium. The term implies that something is remaining unchanged over some period of time. What this something is remains vague in most social theories of equilibrium. But, if the concept is to be used at all, that which is stable must be spelled out factually. Otherwise, we are back to the vacuity of "other things being equal," or empirical claims that can never be refuted (for we never know when other things *are* equal until we are told what they are). In like fashion, we do not know if equilibrium obtains unless we know what factual states are said to be unchanging.

The determination of system boundaries indicates one dimension of the equilibrium problem, for boundaries do not change in terms of what phenomena are to be included in the system. Establishing boundaries also reveals how the notion of equilibrium must be handled. When we construct definitional criteria for system limits, what are held constant are the definitions. Events come and go, and relationships alter over time. But our conceptualization of phenomena as a system remains the same. This conceptual stability avoids two common errors in system equilibrium: first, that a state of equilibrium is in any sense natural or desirable; second, that events tend to move toward equilibrium. A system is nothing more than a model to order phenomena (not a real property of the social universe).

But to be operative, the criteria for including phenomena in a system must be specifically defined. Since the political system is a smaller class within the social system, any general treatment of system boundaries must begin with an investigation of social systems. Talcott Parsons remains the definitive figure in contemporary systems theory, in part because of the seemingly exhaustive categorical apparatus he has constructed to order modes of behavior, but also because he continues the Weberian emphasis on conceptualization from the viewpoint of the actor instead of the analyst. Parsons' social system is the interactive relationships of a plurality of individual actors, who are defined in terms of their own orientations.[18]

Any situation (for Parsons) provides two major classes of objects to which an actor may be oriented: nonsocial (physical objects and the like) and social (individual actors and collectivities). The orientations of actors to these two kinds of objects can be either cognitive, cathectic, or evaluative. A cognitive discrimination is the selection of objects which are available in a given situation. The tendency to react positively or negatively to objects is the cathectic mode of orientation, while the process of assessing objects in terms of their ramified consequences is called evaluation.[19]

Two observations must be made here. First, this conceptualization of a social system involves units which are interacting in a state of mutual dependence, but the units are taken from the inside. It is not overt behavior which is referred to, but the subjective meanings of human beings. Three major classes of cultural patterns correspond to the three types of orientation: ideas or beliefs (cognition), expressive symbols (cathexis), and value-orientations (evaluation). All may be seen as subjective perspectives. Second, the system that Parsons constructs is an action system. By

[18] Talcott Parsons and Edward Shils, eds., *Toward a General Theory of Action* (New York: Harper & Row, 1962), pp. 3–27.
[19] *Ibid.*

this is meant that change occurs in the orientations of actors, although—again—the definitions of the concepts remain the same.

All human action, for Parsons, is goal-oriented. This refers both to individual and collective behavior, which are constituted by the same concrete processes (even though the personality is independent by virtue of its specific biological patterns and life history). Further, all action systems have certain functional imperatives, which may be conceptualized as pattern maintenance, goal attainment, adaptation, and integration. Maintenance of patterns is the positive continuance of the system's value framework. The system also must control situations to allow for objects to be secured by individuals and collectivities (within the limits of the prevailing value pattern). Finally, a social system must adjust to its environment and maintain solidarity in the relations between system units.

From this brief account we can see that social phenomena, for Parsons, are the totality of orientations of human beings living in society, where a society is a factual system which contains within itself all the essential prerequisites for self-subsistence (territorial location; a process for determining functions and allocating facilities and rewards; and integrative structures controlling these allocations and regulating conflicts). This establishment of boundaries is more embracing than precise, but this is not Parsons' major problem. Social data, after all, are eclectic to begin with, for the term can refer to all subsystems (politics, economics, etc.) in a geographical area.

The central difficulty with the Parsonian model is a peculiar bias which we shall have occasion to refer to again later. We may, as a way of explaining this bias, view a social system either in terms of an integration model, which stresses agreement among members, or a coercion model, which emphasizes disagreement. In the first case, the elements of stability, integration, functional coordination, and consensus orient the model. Talcott Parsons operates with this kind of a model. The second model, on the other hand, is based on assumptions of change, conflict, disintegration, and coercion. Marx comes to mind.[20]

Both consensus and conflict are present within any society. Focusing on one to the exclusion of the other distorts systems analysis. This is precisely the bias built into the Parson tradition in systems models. In fairness to Parsons, however, the construction of any societal model entails conceptual stability. Even Marx works with patterns of conflict which are amenable to a lawlike presentation in his model. It is the old tension between conceptual order and the open dimensions of the world. But, on the other hand, one cannot transfer conceptual requirements to the phenomena without distortion entering the analysis. To assume, as Parsons does, that empirical societies must be seen in terms of maintaining activities is to ignore the more radical forces pressing for disintegration.

Boundaries: Political Systems

The natural eclecticism of social phenomena cannot be tolerated in those subsystems within the larger social framework. While social data may be taken, as we have seen, as the composite orientations of human beings living in a self-subsistent area, the economic or political system must be separated out from the general social aggregate. This task reduces to the question of determining what special features some social events possess which entitle them to be called economic or political. Hence, additional distinctions must be made within the social system that will yield the subsystems we seek.

Attempts to define political events are hardly new enterprises. Aristotle defined the state as that which aims at the

[20] Ralf Dahrendorf, *Class and Class Conflict in Industrial Society* (Stanford, Calif.: Stanford University Press, 1959), pp. 160–63.

AND ESSAYS.

highest good. Definitions including norms, however, have been considered prosaic since Weber, who conceptualized the state as that agency possessing ultimate force in a given territory. Force as used by Weber can be either illegitimate (power) or legitimate (authority). The forms of authority in Weber's schema are well known: traditional, charismatic, and legal.[21] What Weber attempted to do is clear. By focusing on those events which participate in the exercise of ultimate force, we have conceptualized the political arena.

More modern attempts to define political phenomena remain within Weber's methodological axioms on value, but often engage different kinds of phenomena as a way of identifying political systems. Karl Deutsch, for example, identifies the political in terms of communication. With this concept a political system can be distinguished by the rate and kind of information exchanges occurring in a territory.[22] Perhaps the most widely known modern definition of political phenomena, however, remains that posited by David Easton. For Easton, politics is the authoritative allocation of values.[23] This can be taken to mean policy which is binding for all or most members of a society in the sense that people feel they must or ought to obey the policy, even though its effective range may be limited to a few members of society directly.[24]

The advantages of this definition are obvious enough. Most certainly it establishes the boundaries of a political system, which are in this case the web of actions which

[21] Max Weber, *The Theory of Social and Economic Organization* (Glencoe, Ill.: The Free Press, 1964), p. 328.

[22] Karl Deutsch, *Nationalism and Social Communication* (Cambridge: Massachusetts Institute of Technology Press, 1966), and *The Nerves of Government* (New York: The Free Press, 1966).

[23] Easton, *The Political System* (New York: Alfred A. Knopf, 1959), pp. 129–34.

[24] Ibid., p. 134. See also Easton's discussion in one of his later works, *A Framework for Political Analysis* (Englewood Cliffs, N.J.: Prentice-Hall, 1965), pp. 47–75.

authoritatively allocate values for society. Other favorable features have been richly discussed: it focuses on activity instead of institutions, which cannot always be said of the use of the state as a conceptual instrument; it escapes the definitional morass of power; and it provides a general framework for locating political variables which is more elegant than the various versions of equilibrium theory, and more comprehensive than the group approach. All of these characteristics have been examined at great length in the literature.

But, as we might expect, the definition has its problems also. For one thing, the choice of value as a key term is an unfortunate one. It is a relational concept and really cannot be allocated.[25] It needs both subject and object, and the value of an object is not an intrinsic property of the object but rather a derivative of the needs and desires of the subject.[26] However, this point should not be pushed too far, for the problem is only a terminological one which could be alleviated without too much difficulty. We might, that is, take the definition as one which refers simply to decisions which deny things to some people and make them accessible to others, and not to a relational concept which is an unlikely candidate for the quantification implied in the notion of allocation.

The more acute difficulties come about as the implications of the definition are unraveled. To remain consistent, we must exclude a number of policy decisions made by governments which do not quite fit the proposal. Marginal cases are frequent. Many decisions of legally constituted officials do not deny things and make things accessible except in the remotest sense of allocation. We may take the issue of a new stamp as an example. Of course, it *is* possible to argue that in a strict sense the use of material and labor to make

[25] William Mitchell, "Politics as the Allocation of Value: A Critique," *Ethics* (1961), pp. 79–89.

[26] See the later discussion in Chapter V.

the stamp constitutes a form of allocation. This would be consistent with the qualification that binding policy does not have to affect people directly. The example is used here only to demonstrate that allocation embraces an extraordinarily wide range of events, from the superficial to the most serious.

Other policy decisions of government are not so easily subsumed under the definition. The classic separation of policy-making levels of government produces directives which do not even in intent apply to all of society, and in fact often conflict with one another in the same societal areas. Again, the qualification that only a few need to be directly affected by policy provides an escape for the existence of regional policies, but the specter of conflicting policy is not so easily eluded. One cannot, after all, say of antagonistic policies that they are or are not authoritative for all or most members of a society except by the introduction of other criteria for authoritative, for people may be in disagreement about what policy ought to be obeyed. The whole problem of civil rights in the United States comes to mind. Even more serious for the definition is a policy, such as Prohibition, which perhaps people feel they ought *not* to obey.

The fundamental problem here is an implicit assumption that policy is a seamless web toward which the public can respond in a positive or negative fashion, when in reality both policy and public response are pluralistic. At the very least, policy as used here is comprised of both decisions and implementations. But we may on occasion wish to view decisions which are *not* implemented (by either enforcement or acceptance) as quite political. Further, people may have ambivalent feelings toward decisions which are enforced, even to the point where these decisions do not result in compulsion to obey in any degree.

Two possibilities of meeting these objections are open, neither one wholly satisfactory. First, one can (by fiat) exclude from the category of the political all decisions of government which people do not feel they ought to obey for one reason or another. But by doing this one has brought into the political system the consensus bias which characterizes Parsons' work. To be sure, Easton allows for the possibility that people may feel that they must or ought to obey policy on any one of a number of grounds, including coercion. But if the definition of policy is confined to the affirmation of the public, whatever the reasons for the affirmation, then nonaffirmed government decisions of two crucial sorts cannot be explained: those which are promulgated and not enforced, and those which are promulgated and enforced on an unwilling public. With affirmation, therefore, two important kinds of policy emerging from social dissonance remain outside the model.

The other way in which pluralistic policies and responses can be dealt with is by introducing additional means for determining when policy is to be considered authoritative. The most common avenue taken here is to construct a legitimacy continuum for separating general policy from legitimately grounded policy. In such a schema, the question of consent would be peripheral to that of whether or not the policy is legitimate. Authoritative policy might be considered that which is legitimate, regardless of whether or not the members of society feel at any given moment that they ought to obey the policy at issue.[27] If the ghost of Weber appears to be embodied in this, we should not be overly surprised. The whole notion, after all, of ultimately binding policy is curiously reminiscent of another dead concept: sovereignty. On the other hand, if such a continuum were in fact introduced into Easton's concept, then the basic attempt to avoid the tortuous distinctions separating power and authority has failed.

[27] This is what Gabriel Almond et al., have done by defining the political system as a system of interactions performing the functions of integration and adaptation by means of the employment, or threat of employment, of more or less legitimate physical compulsion. See Politics of the Developing Areas (Princeton, N.J.: Princeton University Press, 1960), pp. 3–64.

That these distinctions *are* tortuous can be easily demonstrated. Legitimacy can be established from one of two directions: either from the viewpoint of actors in the given social system, or from the vantage point of a standard independent of the social system in question. In the first case, criteria which are indigenous to a culture must be weighed and considered, which opens the door to conflicting judgments by various cultural groups. It also reopens the consensus bias alluded to earlier. In the second case, we are confronted with the complex task of adequately justifying an independent standard or norm. Enough has already been said about *this* problem. Establishing legitimacy is a monumental task precisely because it involves the determination of correct behavior, and aside from the status quo itself we have no readily available standard to secure such a determination.

If this account seems overly critical, it should not be so taken. The notion of binding decisions is the key concept in abstracting the political system from social phenomena, and Easton's imaginative concept has freed us from the stalemate of institutional analysis while remaining within the classic rubric of obligation in political behavior. But we would do well to refine the definition of political events to include both coercive and nonenforced policy. Aside from the two obvious alternatives mentioned above, a more complex (but perhaps fruitful) avenue to accomplish this might be the inclusion of *all* decisions made by government officials. Added to the concept of public response, the kinds of political events currently excluded from the Easton framework would be treated. This expansion would entail the incorporation of institutional data, but formal structures cannot be wholly ignored in any case (as Easton points out).

An even more radical alternative would be a theory which is based not on the political system, but on political *systems*. In this approach, any social system would be seen as containing a mosaic of political systems, each defined in terms of the changing relationships between the orientations of

actors (whether people feel they ought to obey a government directive or not) and the decisions which government
officials make. In this way pluralism could be introduced into
Easton's more monolithic concept of policy.[28] Whether this
would be operationally more advantageous would depend on
the theoretical possibilities of connecting the attitude states
and official decisions in one systematic framework.

Function and Structure

Other problems in functional analysis derive from the relationship of two basic concepts: function and structure.
Both are used inconsistently in the literature. For Marion
Levy, a function is a condition, or state of affairs, resultant
from the operation of a structure through time. This may be
taken to be *what* exists. A structure is a pattern of action, or
the framework through which functions operate.[29] That is,
given that certain processes are fulfilled, say the distribution
of goods and services to the public, then these processes are
functions, and *how* these processes are carried out is the
structure of society. In this case, goods and services may be
distributed, let us say, either through the framework of a
political machine or of the federal government. The temptation is to use structure and system synonymously, but, as
we shall see, this cannot be done in political systems.

For Merton, a function is an observable objective consequence, which can, in turn, be either manifest or latent.
Manifest functions are those which are intended and recognized by actors in the system, while latent functions are

[28] Easton relaxes his definition of political phenomena in *A Framework for Political Analysis, op. cit.* See page 50 for a definition of system boundaries as social interactions *predominantly* oriented toward the
authoritative allocation of values for a society. This leaves open the
possibility of including some of the themes indicated here.

[29] Marion Levy, "Some Aspects of 'Structural-Functional' Analysis
and Political Science," in Roland Young, ed., *Approaches to the Study
of Politics* (Evanston, Ill.: Northwestern University Press, 1958).

those neither intended nor recognized. To be precise, Merton reserves the term function for those consequences making for the adaptation or adjustment of a given system. Dysfunctions, accordingly, lessen adaptation or adjustment, and nonfunctional consequences are irrelevant to the system under examination. This distinction between positive and negative consequences makes sense of the manifest–latent dichotomy; for manifest functions are simply the congruence of actor-purpose with positive consequences, and latent functions are those positive consequences which are not a part of actor-purpose. The manifest–latent dichotomy also is applicable to dysfunctions and nonfunctions.[30]

The trouble with Merton's paradigm is in the notion of consequence. What is attempted with this concept is admirable enough, which is a direct link between functional unit and system state. But, unfortunately, the term consequence means a result, which entails an antecedent event. Defining and examining the event preceding the function thus becomes a requirement. The paradigm in question does not handle this. With Levy's use we get no separation between event and result, but, conversely, neither do we get a direct relationship between function and collectivity. The problem here is defining function in such a way that it is overtly related to the concept of system (which is a necessity in functional analysis), while at the same time not ignoring the event for the sake of the result. This means that the two fundamental properties of function must be merged: event and consequent.

The concept of structure is vital to political systems. If we pursue Easton's definition of the political, then a political system must always perform at least one function, the authoritative allocation of values. This means, further, that structure, as the way in which this basic function is carried out, is definitive in distinguishing one political system from an-

---

[30] Merton, *op. cit. Social Theory and Social Structure*, pp. 51–54.

other. The authoritative allocation of values cannot change as long as the political system remains in existence. What changes is the form or structure implementing this function. The question of democracy or authoritarianism is a question of structure, not of function.

Other functions exist, of course, in the political world. James Prothro has constructed a model of a political system which synthesizes and improves on the general suggestions of recent years, and which demonstrates the kinds of activities taken as political functions. Functional categories are broken down into input functions and output functions. Within these two general classes, specification is made of identifiable activities by which these functions are realized. Inputs are demands, supports, and apathy,[31] while a specification of these are leadership selection and interest identification.[32] The output functions are rewards and deprivations, which can be translated into rule making, settlement of disputes, and rule application.[33] The specifications are narrower instances of the two more general functions labeled input and output.

But, even with this specification of functions, we cannot say that the question of political structures has been answered. In one sense, of course, we have delineated *how* in-

---

[31] Easton does not include apathy, but this variable can be functional or dysfunctional along with the two categories of demands and supports. For example, electoral surveys in the United States have demonstrated that the most apathetic voters also tend to be the least informed and the most antilibertarian. Hence the fact that this group does not participate in politics may be considered functional for a democratic polity.

[32] This represents a merger of Almond's four categories of political socialization and recruitment, interest articulation, interest aggregation, and political communication.

[33] Almond's output functions are rule making, rule application, and rule adjudication. All of the ideas for these changes in the Easton and Almond models come from Professor Prothro's *The Politics of American Democracy* (with Marian Irish) (Englewood Cliffs, N.J.: Prentice-Hall, 1965).

puts (demands, supports, apathy) are conducted by referring to leadership selection and interest identification. But such a reference remains within the *what* category, for all we have done is move to a more specific (or operational) level of the same class of items. To answer the question of *how* functions are carried out suggests that features even more specific have to be denoted. All societies select leaders and identify interests. Therefore we have not indicated the form in which functions are realized by alluding to this generality.

The distinction gotten at here can be demonstrated with a previously used example. Inputs may be taken as the posture of actors toward their political system, while outputs denote the system's posture toward the actors. Let us say that a group of actors desires certain foodstuffs to keep alive. We have not said anything about the way in which this demand is realized when we indicate that the system identifies the given interest and selects certain leaders, for this is included in the definition of a political system. However, if we say that a system possesses a political machine through which this demand operates, then we have answered the question of *how* functions are realized.

If we pursue this distinction between function as a general condition and structure as a specific pattern of activities, then we have a means of distinguishing factual political systems from each other as well as a model to represent all empirical political systems. Structure defined in this way is the specific embodiment of function in each society. But this means that structure cannot be thought of as the fixed relationship among system parts, for it must be essentially malleable.[34] What changes in and between political systems is the structure; the functions remain constant. This is straightforward enough, inasmuch as structural terms are factual and

[34] The notion of structure as a fixed relationship is, unfortunately, a common one. This is claimed by, among others, H. Blalock and A. Blalock, "Toward a Clarification of Systems Analysis in the Social Sciences," *Philosophy of Science* XXVI (1959), pp. 84–92.

functional terms are abstract classes. So too are the implications: the idea of structures as static properties must be discarded if functional analysis in political inquiry is to be consistent.

The use of the concept "structure" also obviates a common criticism of functional analysis, which is that it does not explain anything because the *explanans* and the *explanan-duum* are synonymous.[35] Moliere's satire comes to mind: opium puts people to sleep because it possesses a dormant character. This absurdity is avoided by introducing structures as the factual range of functions. Political systems are then defined by functional generalities (which may be seen as judgments by the analyst about the way in which events are related to each other), and explanation is conducted at the factual (or structural) level between specific sets of events and a specified range of system variables.

System States

The final problem in functional analysis is specifying a satisfactorily operating system. Merton, we will recall, defines function in terms of consequences for the adaptation or adjustment of a system. Parsons means by function a contribution to the maintenance or development of a system.[36] This depiction of function in terms of a satisfactory system state is universal to functional theory. Two themes are suggested by this view, both of which have emerged in earlier discussions. One is that of defining a satisfactory system state as the fulfillment of actor-goals. The other is the claim that grounds exist for determining satisfactory functioning which are independent of actor-goals. In all of the definitions of function the question of what constitutes a

[35] For example, see Robert Dowse, "A Functionalist's Logic," *World Politics* (July 1966), pp. 607–22.

[36] Parsons and Shils, eds. *op. cit.*, *Toward A General Theory Of Action.*

smoothly operating system must be answered by one of these two approaches.

Each of the two grounds for answering this question have well-known difficulties. If one relies entirely on actor-goals, then one is confronted with the perennial dilemmas of immediate versus long-range satisfactions, as well as the difficulty of dissonance. The latter difficulty means that some events will always be functional for parts of the system and dysfunctional for others. Also, this view commits one to the absurdity that what actors desire is always functional for the ongoing social system. On the other hand, the construction of independent grounds for a satisfactory system opens the door for the biases of the analysts, along with the uncertainties seemingly built into value arguments of this sort.

Yet the specification has to be made. Otherwise functional analysis lapses into feeble tautologies of the sort, event X is functional for smoothly working system Y, and system Y is smoothly working because event X is present. To avoid such mistakes, the specific conditions defining the operating norms of the system under consideration must be made explicit. Otherwise the whole notion of function as an event–system relationship is lost, as well as the entire range of claims for system prerequisites.

Two alternative responses to this requirement might be pursued. One is to construct a hierarchy of human needs which are universal. In this way we would be able to ground purposes which would be independent of any given actor-goals, and the degree to which these needs are fulfilled would then be adequate criteria for assessing the functional contributions of specific events. The enormous problems in constructing such a hierarchy should be obvious. However, this approach is becoming more prominent in the literature.

H.L.A. Hart, for example, advances what he calls the minimum content of natural law. These are universal characteristics of human nature which are necessary in the sense that society could not further the purpose of survival without taking them into account. They are (1) human vulnerability, (2) approximate equality, (3) limited altruism, (4) limited resources, and (5) limited understanding and strength of will.[37] Notice that these universal standards are more relevant in determining dysfunctions (behavior that violates these characteristics) than in identifying functional activity. They are, that is, necessary but not sufficient norms for a satisfactory social system.

A. H. Maslow has made a more positive identification of universal standards. What he claims is an empirically verifiable hierarchy of human needs which can be used to assess behavior as functional or dysfunctional for the long-range (ultimate?) good of a social system. They are, in order of their assumed priority: (1) physical needs, (2) safety needs, (3) belongingness and love needs, (4) esteem needs, (5) need for self-actualization and growth, and (less important) (6) the need to know and understand, and, finally, (7) aesthetic needs.[38] Christian Bay has urged the adoption of such universals to guide modern political science research.[39]

Only the two most obvious problems with this approach will be mentioned here. First, the move from factual needs to normative standards can only be carried out by the use of a hidden premise, viz, that human needs *ought* to be satisfied. This is a modest enough assumption, but we should know that it exists. A half-century of theorists have criticized the utilitarians for not realizing that the proposition "X causes the greatest happiness, but it is not good" is *not* self-contradictory. Made explicit, this hidden premise pushes

[37] H.L.A. Hart, *The Concept of Law* (Oxford: Clarendon Press, 1961), pp. 190–93.

[38] A. H. Maslow, *Motivation and Personality* (New York: Harper & Row, 1954), pp. 80–106. Also see Maslow's *Toward a Psychology of Being* (New York: D. Van Nostrand Co., 1962).

[39] Christian Bay, "Politics and Pseudopolitics: A Critical Evaluation of Some Behavioral Literature," *American Political Science Review*, March, 1965, pp. 39–51.

the claim more toward the ontological thesis of Albert Camus, who argues in *The Myth of Sisyphus* that existence *qua* existence is good. Again, this is not a shameful alliance, but neither is it the clear empirical presentation which its adherents make it out to be.

Second, the categories of needs are themselves essentially vacuous. Hart escapes this and the former criticism by laying out only the limits beyond which social directives cannot go without destroying the common purpose of survival which men share in associating with each other. But the positive exhortations of Maslow and Bay open up other requirements, such as what specifically is to constitute the satisfaction of love needs, or needs for esteem. It has not been the abstract voiding of such hierarchies that has distinguished tyrants, but how they factually defined such human requirements. Sadly enough, both Hitler and Ghandi can be comfortably housed within Maslow's general framework.

The alternative to human needs as a basis for standards yielding satisfactory or nonsatisfactory system states is to construct criteria for system norms which are, in a sense, arbitrary. By this we mean instrumental frameworks to be utilized or discarded as they serve explanatory roles posited by the analyst. The problem with this option is obvious: any explanation would be fundamentally ephemeral, which is the classic dilemma of any escape from norm universality. The bland mix of this solution is also classic, for what we have in such an approach is a set of system states which determine functional and dysfunctional behavior only in a manner which is internal to the conceptual scheme. Whether these relationships correspond to real human needs is entirely random.

The two themes of actor-goals and independent standards have been with us from the dialogue on classical and modern political theory, and we will have much more to say about them later. Even, however, with one or the other as a definitional standard for system states, we still face the question of whether a specific event can in any case be related functionally to an entire system. As we saw earlier, systems with any degree of pluralism may take events functionally in one context and dysfunctionally in another. The question is whether we can speak of events as functional except in specific contexts considerably narrower than the whole system. But without standards of either actor-orientation or independent genre, not even in contexts can we call events functional or dysfunctional. Therefore one or the other source of standards must be chosen. Whichever one is selected indicates a great deal about the value-orientation of functional analysis.

CHAPTER IV

Science and Social Analysis

THE SCIENTIFIC WELTANSCHAUUNG

Science is both myth and reality. This in itself is neither here nor there, inasmuch as most things in the world are also. But the peculiar myth of science is that it dispenses with all myths. The picture of the unbiased scientist in pursuit of objective truth is both well known and commonly accepted. It is too much (as we have seen) to assume that the facts speak for themselves. But, ideally, the scientist is taken as one who attaches himself only skeptically to one point of view or another. Like most myths this one consists of a mixture of truth and exaggeration. The problem is determining the exact ratio of the ingredients.

At the level of general theory the common image of science is stretched the thinnest. Instead of unattached activity we get firm commitment. Thomas Kuhn paints a picture of the scientific enterprise in *The Structure of Scientific Revo-*

lutions[1] which is worth outlining in some detail. For Kuhn, most science is conducted within a rigid view of the world vigorously defended by those adhering to it; and the adherents are composed of the general scientific community. Kuhn allows for exceptions, however, and these exceptions represent the creative breaks with the past which lead (eventually) to scientific revolutions. Hence the salient distinction for Kuhn is between normal science, which is defined as the perfunctory verification of the dominant theoretical framework in any historical period; and extraordinary science, which is the abrupt development of a rival theoretical framework, and which can only be accepted gradually by the scientific community.

Instead of unbiased skeptics, we get a picture of partisans defending the established order. However, we must not take the established order as only a hindrance to research. It is also a necessity. Kuhn defines this order as a paradigm, meaning the agreement on theory, problem areas, and techniques which characterizes normal science. Without a paradigm, scientific research could not take place as a collective enterprise, for science needs an organizing principle. A paradigm fulfills this requirement at all levels, from the simple task of defining facts to the broader role of establishing criteria for recognizing problems and research approaches. The paradigm *is* the commonality underlying a scientific community.

Paradigms are, however, rejected. This is what is revolutionary about science. The process of rejection begins as the paradigm is verified; for as scientists factually prove various dimensions of the general theory in a paradigm, the congruence of theory and data becomes more tenuous. Put another way, the general theory is found to fit the world less easily as it is pressed more thoroughly against the world. These anomalies become more recognizable as verification

[1] Kuhn, *The Structure of Scientific Revolutions* (Chicago: University of Chicago Press, 1962).

continues. At some point a rival candidate for general theory is constructed. Disagreement ensues between the supporters of old and new theory, culminating finally in the acceptance of the new paradigm and the reestablishment of normal research.

Kuhn is quick to point out the recalcitrance of scientists toward paradigm change. Part of this recalcitrance is manifest in the seeming inability of most people to perceive anomalies right away. In one experiment (cited by Kuhn) conducted by J. S. Bruner and Leo Postman, subjects were asked to identify anomalous playing cards, such as red clubs, black hearts, and the like. Almost all the subjects identified the cards on short exposure as normal, suggesting that what was perceived was easily slipped into mental categories established prior to experience. More exposure to the cards brought recognition of anomaly, but some subjects could not correctly identify the cards at 40 times the average exposure required to recognize normal cards.[2]

The conclusion to be drawn from experiments like this is that we see what we come to see. At the level of a paradigm, such behavior produces a kind of scientific lag. Long after a general theory has failed to correspond to phenomena, it remains as the accepted approach; for anomalies are simply subsumed under the accepted theoretical categories—either because they are missed altogether (as the playing cards were above) or because they are explained away as isolated errors in measurement. In this way the necessary function of a conceptual scheme in defining facts turns out to be a liability when the paradigm's failures to fit the world call for a replacement.

Yet, as Kuhn points out, novelty cannot be defined except in terms of an established framework; for anomalies are departures from the normal continuity of experience. Thus the unusual event which signifies the need for a new theory

[2] J. S. Bruner and Leo Postman, "On the Perception of Incongruity: a Paradigm," *Journal of Personality*, XVIII (1949), pp. 206–23.

can only be perceived by someone who knows thoroughly what to expect, and hence recognizes that something has gone wrong. Without a paradigm, phenomena are described differently by different men and no facts (as we think of facts in terms of general acceptance) exist. So partisanship is a necessary condition for creativity, even though it is in purpose antagonistic to it.

The ambiguity expected in paradigm replacement is twofold. The discreditation of a general theory leads to uncertainty, but uncertainty also enters the discrediting process. Anomalies of one sort or another always occur, for theories never totally fit the world. This means that scientists can never be sure that the errors they encounter in verifying a theory are indicative of a general inadequacy in the theory. This also helps to explain the reluctance with which scientists discard paradigms. Kuhn points out that individuals engaged in normal research are in any case not congenitally prone to reflect on their deeper preconceptions. This amounts to the virtually self-evident truth that philosophy is of little use in the laboratory.

Once a replacement process begins, however, then an uncertainty on the legitimate paradigm splits the scientific community. This is the period that Kuhn calls extraordinary science. It is characterized by random research, philosophical analysis, and accidental discoveries. Aimless laboratory work combines with intellectual reflection on what science is all about. Two cautionary notes: First, partisan support of one or another paradigm is the main feature of scientific revolutions, not vague drifting without commitment. Second, the discarding of one paradigm is always carried out with the acceptance of another. Order is not long absent from the scientific enterprise.

✿   ✿   ✿

What we are to make of Kuhn's provocative thesis turns on the range of validity we want to ascribe to it. As a factual description of the change pattern in the physical sciences, it is both correct and enlightening. But if taken as a statement of the necessary pattern of all scientific research, a dissent can be voiced. The dissent can be framed in terms of the contingent relationship of the two kinds of science in Kuhn's description—normal and extraordinary—to the existence or nonexistence of a paradigm.

The initial question is whether science can be conducted in any fashion without a paradigm. This is a point of ambivalence for Kuhn. On the one hand a paradigm is crucial in establishing priorities for research and standards for defining facts. On the other hand a transient kind of inquiry called extraordinary science is possible. But, if we take seriously the notion of a paradigm as a community consensus on method and corpus, then extraordinary science is without a paradigm. What is characteristic of this revolutionary period is conflicting general theories (no one of which has assumed the status of a paradigm). However, does not scientific research go on during periods of extraordinary science?

Kuhn would probably allow that it does, reserving the necessity of a paradigm to the conduct of normal science. But regardless of such a response, the question itself may be directed to normal science; for if normal science can be conducted on a level that is more specific than a paradigm and independent of it, then the role of community consensus diminishes in logical importance (although it still retains traditional importance). We must ask, that is, how tightly we are to link all normal science to paradigm-directed research.

This is a question which can never be settled definitively by relying on the historical development of the physical sciences. What gives Kuhn's thesis its weight is the close factual association of ordinary science with a paradigm. But the outlines of a separation can be discerned when the thesis is extended factually beyond the physical sciences, for Kuhn's definition of normal research is not simply a synonym for the existence of a paradigm. If it were, of course, then no separation would be conceivable. But features not included in the meaning of a paradigm are ascribed to normal research, among these the characteristics of puzzle-solving, matching facts with theory, determination of significant facts, and articulation of theory.[3]

The question is whether all or some of these characteristics can be found in scientific inquiry which lacks a paradigm. If so, then much of what Kuhn takes as normal science would not be *logically* connected to the existence of a paradigm. The social sciences (as one might expect) furnish more instances of seemingly normal research conducted in this way. Political analysis has been distinguished in recent years by the appearance of several middle-range theories, such as group theory. To use a group as the conceptual unit of study is to stay well below the threshold of a paradigm. Yet scientific research is conducted in this narrower approach; and it can hardly be called extraordinary.

It is true that facts can only be defined within some conceptual scheme. But the issue posed here is the generality of the conceptual scheme. Political investigators who verify forms of group theory need not agree on a general theory of politics, indicating that the activity which constitutes normal research (such as puzzle-solving, and the like) is compatible with the absence of a paradigm. The agreement directing specific inquiry may exist only within certain fragments of the scientific population, and rest simply on narrow-gauge theory. This same inversion of activity and paradigm presence can be gotten out of Kuhn's case for extraordinary science (although with far less persuasiveness); for instances of random research, philosophical analysis, and accidental discoveries can also occur within a paradigm.

Again, the factual association of activity with its appropriate paradigm state is extremely close in the physical sci-

[3] *Op. cit.*, pp. 33, 35–42.

ences. But the association *is* factual, and not necessary. Therefore several qualifications to Kuhn's account of science must be kept in mind. First, the relationship of research to the existence of a paradigm may vary from one branch of the physical sciences to another, moving from the strong "normal science–paradigm" and "extraordinary science–no paradigm" relationships Kuhn postulates to any one of a number of ambiguous positions along the continuum over to the antithesis of Kuhn's account: "normal science–no paradigm" and "extraordinary science–paradigm." Second, as a historical account of scientific development, future research patterns may modify it. Third, any transfer of Kuhn's thesis from the physical to the social sciences may have to encounter factual evidence even more antagonistic to it than anything found in the physical sciences; and as a factual thesis it must change in accordance with new evidence.

THE SCIENTIFIC METHOD

What remains of Kuhn's thesis is formidable enough: the pursuit of science is consistent with intellectual partisanship. This partisanship, however, is the general theoretical framework within which scientific research takes place. The question of neutrality v. commitment must therefore be asked at a narrower level. Is it possible to maintain the ideal skepticism of science after the general point of view has been established? This query is directed at the concrete level of securing evidence and weighing it in terms of narrow propositions. Given that we may be biased in a large way, that is, can we be neutral in a small way?

Whether scientists *are* skeptical truth-seekers at the operational level cannot be answered with a theoretical discussion. To establish this would entail a factual inquiry into the hard practice of science. But it is possible in theoretical discourse to define neutrality. In such a definition we can engage what would be necessary *if* science is to be a bipartisan activity, and what is impossible to secure given some of the conceptual requirements of all inquiry. Whether this definition is factually realized or not is another matter. All that a conceptual analysis can determine is what *can* be realized.

Conceptual discussions of science sooner or later settle on the topic loosely called "the scientific method." We need not believe that in the actual practice of science any formalized procedure is rigidly followed. P. W. Bridgman claimed that "the scientist has no other method than doing his damndest."[4] Nevertheless, a scientific mood or posture can be distinguished on the basis of two basic features: first, the scientific temperament is alleged to be unbiased at the concrete level; second, the conclusions of science are supposed to be capable of verification by any observer who follows the same techniques.

The operational character of science can easily be taken too far. No experiment can be exactly repeated in every way; and so strictly speaking no observer can follow precisely the same techniques. The verification requirements of science amount to the looser thesis of public validation, meaning that under normal circumstances any unbiased observer will come to similar conclusions. What constitutes normal circumstances in the laboratory or field is determined by the scientific community. This means that there can be both good and bad science, depending on the standards of exactness which are in use. But it also means that science cannot function without standards of some kind which define the process of verification, even though exact reproduction of an experiment is impossible.

Scientific knowledge is based on the assumption that circumstances *are* generally normal. This is a wider use of "normal," denoting what Arnold Brecht calls "intersubjectivity,"[5] or the assumption that people see the world in

---

[4] Quoted in Abraham Kaplan's *The Conduct of Inquiry* (San Francisco: Chandler Publishing Co., 1964), p. 27.

[5] Brecht, *Political Theory* (Princeton: Princeton University Press, 1959).

roughly the same way. The burden of the scientific establishment is separating out the normal circumstances of scientific verification from the normal assumptions in the larger
world of general experience; for while science is based on
the common framework of human beings, its claims to exactness rely on a more rigorous procedure for generating
knowledge which is taken as publicly validated by scientists.

Brecht lists, with wistful results, the steps of the scientific
method: (1) observation, (2) description, (3) measurement,
(4) acceptance, (5) inductive generalization, (6) explanation,
(7) deductive reasoning, (8) testing, (9) correcting, (10) predicting, (11) nonacceptance.[6] The only sensible way to take
this delineation is as a conceptual idea to which scientists
aspire, even if at times obliquely; for, again, we have no
reason to think that any tightly-drawn set of steps accurately
represents the conduct of science. But while scientists may
only aspire to Brecht's neat outline, the idea conveyed by
a scientific method is crucial: *some* agreed-upon procedure
must standardize scientific inquiry.

The result of this reliance on procedural standards which
are superimposed on the assumption of intersubjectivity is
that scientific knowledge must be taken in a dual fashion.
On the one hand, it is more certain for those who engage in
science than the commonsense knowledge of general experience. But, on the other hand, the very nature of procedural checks imposes a problematic tone on scientific
conclusions. They are, in the words of Karl Popper, hypotheses which have resisted disproof.[7] Given, that is, the
paradigm which directs scientific inquiry, the specific statements linking the paradigm to the world are both verified
and always capable of falsification.

The absence of bias in scientific procedure is even more
difficult to define than normal circumstances. Neutrality
certainly does not entail a conceptual steam bath leading to

[6] *Ibid.*, pp. 28–29.

[7] Popper, *The Logic of Scientific Discovery*. (New York: Harper
& Row, 1959).

a state of intellectual purity in the tradition of Locke's *tabula rasa*. As we have seen (cf. Chapter I), all inquiry must take place within an intellectual framework of some kind. A pure, or primordial, sensation is not part of reflective activity. It follows that scientific neutrality involves a set of givens, which are found in every theory. These givens have been discussed earlier as they range from the methodological to general views of the world.

What then is suspended? It is tempting to answer, everything else, but this is misleading. The necessary given of empirical science embraces the larger part; what is placed in abeyance to secure neutrality is a much more modest undertaking. Specific value judgments are to be held aside in science; and this exclusion, essentially, is what is meant by the neutrality of the observer. A separate chapter is devoted to the question of values, so no more need be said now except for this: Neutrality attains meaning *after* the givens of science have been assumed. Only within the conceptual framework does the basic dichotomy of *ought* and *is* exist; and a neutral observer is one who focuses on what *is* the case within his point of view, and not on what *ought* to be the case.

Verification and Falsification

The most obvious remark to make about verification has already been made in the discussion of positivism. Scientific knowledge is that body of conclusions which is accepted by the scientific community; and, to the degree that scientific standards differ from ordinary standards, scientific knowledge differs from ordinary knowledge. This remark escapes the category of truisms only as it yields a separation between genuine knowledge and scientific knowledge; for genuine knowledge can exist (established even scientifically, let us say, in retrospect) which is not considered knowledge by the scientific community at a time when it may be public. Also, there may be personal knowledge which is true, and yet of such a nature that it simply cannot be verified. An example of this is some experience one has while alone for which there is no evidence available to establish a general proof.

The separation between scientific inquiry and the *Lebenswelt* is important precisely because it reveals the circumscription of science. Science is, as we have emphasized, a way of looking at the world which does not exhaust all ways of looking at the world. Further, as a distinct form of inquiry resting on special methods of verification, it is vulnerable to a peculiar but effective critique of all formal modes of inquiry. It goes something like this: The genuineness (or truth, or reliability) of knowledge is a product of the way in which knowledge is verified (or made certain). Yet the method chosen for verification cannot be ultimately verified, for its acceptance is the prior condition for establishing proof.

Notice that this critique grows out of a point we made earlier: that any intellectual position involves some degree of affirmation which is prior to the validation procedures constructed within the position itself. The significance of this point is that it applies to all epistemic claims, and gives a peculiar uncertainty to knowledge *qua* knowledge. The scientific method cannot be verified as *the* correct method with the techniques of science. But, then, neither can any other approach be ultimately grounded. Besides introducing a tenuous note into all procedures of verification, however, this argument demonstrates that substance and method are unavoidably connected. This is especially true of the certainty with which substantive knowledge can be held. But this same circle also affects the *kind* of knowledge secured, for scientific knowledge is by definition a derivative of the verification procedures of science; and, as we shall see, scientific verification is a special way of securing certainty (no matter how the scientific community defines its standards).

One more point must be made on the subject of verification. When we say that scientific knowledge is probable and never certain, the degree of probability is a variable with respect to kinds of statements. Only factual statements about the instances of a scientific law are regarded (in the actual conduct of science) as probable. The abstract statement of a scientific principle, as well as the theoretical inferences drawn in accordance with the principle, are framed in *necessary* form.[8] All scientific statements *are* probable in the sense that they must be capable of refutation, but, like Orwell's equality, some are more problematic than others. In the case of certain assumptions, for example the thesis that the universe is finite, we cannot even imagine how refutation is to take place. But assumptions of this sort must be weighed against future evidence, for the skepticism of an empiricist epistemology (though unevenly distributed) must pervade all of science if it is to remain consistent.

SOCIAL PHENOMENA

Whether the study of man can be a science or not is bound up with the philosophical frameworks we have already encountered. The continuity between positivism and the natural sciences engenders one point of view, which is that the methods of the natural sciences are appropriate and efficacious in the study of social phenomena. This argument may be called naturalism. In opposition to this is subjectivism (whose philosophical tradition is comprised of continental philosophers like Nietzsche and Husserl instead of the British and American descendants of Hume). The subjectivist assertion is that the study of society must be pursued with techniques peculiar to social phenomena, and that these methods are not continuous with those of the natural sciences.

[8] Stephen Toulmin, *The Philosophy of Science* (New York: Harper & Row, 1953).

One main objection to the use of natural science techniques in the area of cultural phenomena derives from the nature of the object under scrutiny. This is the claim that phenomena involving human agents are different in kind from natural phenomena because human beings play an intentional role in shaping their future, while the things of nature do not do so in the same fashion. Men think and choose; rocks and trees do not; and animals surely do not think and choose like men.

This argument has two important features. The first is the assumption that human beings are choosing creatures. This claim, however, does not have to rely on a defense of free will against determinism. Something else is more basic here, and it goes back to a view of thought as an intentional act; that is, thought as thought *of* something, and never vacuous. Thus it has a kind of directional character to it, something like a claw constantly reaching out and pinching objects. The analogy may be overdrawn, but something of a scuttling or random overtone to this notion is not quite like the deliberation implied in free will. Yet there is a sort of sequence of choices assumed, even if necessary ones, which presents a part of the distinctiveness of human phenomena and gives it that potential threat to accurate prediction not generated by the movement of natural phenomena.

The other dimension to this claim is that men attribute *meaning* to their acts which, again, nature's agents cannot do. This is quite different from the argument grounded in choice, for here the problem does not so much affect prediction as it does understanding what in fact is happening at any given time. If two men are seen exchanging shells, it is said, the meaning of this act is fugitive to any observer not assuming the subjective points of view of the men engaged in the social act; for only as *they* give some meaning to what they do does the event make any real sense at all. This is not true of other events of nature.

Both dimensions of this argument are obviously true insofar as they draw a distinction between natural and cultural phenomena. The problem is ascertaining the significance of the distinction for methodological techniques; or, as the natural scientist would claim, the lack of significance. Determining this in terms of the first instance, that of human volition, is virtually impossible if the argument is to rest on a demonstration that human choice can be factually validated by capricious behavior. It is a daily truth that human beings behave in predictable fashion. What is more, this consistency is a phenomenon which anyone can perceive and which (in itself) is the ground for the existence of human beings in close proximity to each other without sustained confusion.

Yet neither does this constitute an argument against human volition. Part of the reason for this is lodged in the contingent nature of causality: the future will always remain open-ended, or indeterminate by definition. But the main point is that, even with perfect predictability based on perfect knowledge, all that can be demonstrated is either that choice is coincidental with prediction, or that choice is not a salient factor, which can always mean that it is simply not being exercised at the time in question. Prediction is not coincidental with determinism, although the existence of capricious behavior and perfect sociological knowledge would constitute a stronger case for human volition than any argument against it.

The question must remain open at two levels. Determinism in human affairs cannot be conclusively established or refuted; and predictable behavior in the present is no guarantee of consistency for the future. But, even granting this, its bearing on the methods of the natural sciences is still far from clear. No apparent barrier halts the application of scientific techniques to creatures who make choices, even if they act erratically. Only one difficulty comes to mind, and that is the classic argument of the self-fulfilling or self-deny-ing prophecy.[9] This is the claim that human beings, possessed of awareness and the ability to make choices, have it within their power to alter their behavior in accordance with, or contrary to, any given prediction.

On the face of it, this is certainly true. But three critical points bear on this argument. First, the practical significance of this observation diminishes as one moves from the specific to the aggregate, for societies are surely less capable of responding to any stimulus of this sort than is the individual. Second, this argument does not relate to the appropriateness of the scientific method for cultural studies, but only to the advisability of making public the conclusions secured with this (or any) method. Third, and most important of all, this argument still does not negate if–then projections, or those which predict a certain behavior if other specified conditions are fulfilled; and these are among the most important kinds of prediction made in the social sciences.

The problem of subjective meaning is more significant. What is at issue here is a kind of inside property to acts which is not available to the techniques of science; or, at least, not wholly available. This qualification needs to be made because of the possibility of directly penetrating into that meaning constructed by actors involved in an event. It is, after all, entirely feasible to introduce an attitudinal variable which intervenes between sociological data and behavior: one can always ask the participants exchanging shells what meaning they give to their behavior. This does not mean that their answers will ever fully reveal all of the subtleties surrounding every human act, but it does suggest that all meaning need not be completely hidden behind the cloak of subjectivity.

Two distinct but closely related objections to this procedure may be indicated here. The first is that any entrance

[9] Robert Merton, *Social Theory and Social Structure* (Glencoe, Ill.: The Free Press, 1964), pp. 421–36.

into the event, as in this case (presumably) by the analyst, changes the event and thus unavoidably alters the constellation of meanings attached to it. To claim this, of course, is to see the social world in a special way. Most fundamentally it suggests a fabric of mutually interacting variables, none of which can be adequately analyzed without some alteration in the behavior of some or all parts of the system. Heisenberg's atoms come to mind. This is a curious and important view of a social order, but it is easy to overemphasize its relevance. There exist numerous means to compensate for the entrance of the social analyst, many of which are extremely effective.[10] To take this objection in the following fashion is probably more accurate: no analyst can directly view a social event in the real sense of its occurrence, but in his conceptualization of the event he can largely correct the error produced by his own activity.

The second objection follows from the notion of participation. That is, an argument can be made that the scientific method presupposes an objective observer outside the phenomena which he studies, and this is impossible because human events have no outside as do natural phenomena. There is only the inside of subjective meaning, which cannot be transcended by any human being. Even as analyst the individual is a participant, in this case fulfilling a social role common in modern Western society. This argument is similar in form to the claim that a residue of subjective meaning always remains fugitive to any analysis. Indeed, at the beginning they amount to the same thing. But it must be noticed that a much stronger kind of point emerges from a categorical rejection of any outside to human events: the observer vanishes. Subjectivity now becomes the condition for the existence of *any* human experience.

This means that the application of natural science methods is not even of partial utility in the area of cultural phe-

[10] Herbert Hyman, *Survey Design and Analysis* (Glencoe, Ill.: The Free Press, 1955), pp. 149–72.

nomena. More: that general conceptual schemes cannot be used to explain human acts, for any mental construct is lodged within the agent's own sphere of meaning, and thus is not of general utility. We see, as it were, through a glass darkly; and the glass can never be removed. This is, though, a very hard saying. It amounts to a version of the sociology of knowledge, at least in terms of its effect, and in terms of the kinds of criticisms to which it is vulnerable. In this sense it is a familiar argument and only one point need be made again: that the necessity of a viewpoint is denied by almost no one. The real problem turns on the degree to which one can secure publicly validated knowledge, which is by no means synonymous with objective knowledge, or knowledge outside the sphere of human experience; and publicly validated knowledge can be secured even from the inside of subjective meaning.

One other argument of subjectivism is that social events occur in genetic sequences, each of which is unique and therefore not comparable with any other. Because of this, the argument goes, generalized explanations in the naturalistic sense are impossible. The source of uniqueness in human acts is, as we might expect, attributed to the effect of conscious intentions on the part of man. But it is not the unavoidable bias of the analyst which causes the methods of science to break down in the area of cultural data. It is rather the fact that actors in social situations behave in specific and incomparable fashions.

Notice that this argument differs from the traditional polemic against positivism, which is that history cannot be repeated in a laboratory experiment like, say, the heating of gases to measure pressure changes, and thus is not amenable to the theoretical conclusions of science. In this case, the lack of similarity is a strong point for the subjectivist position, for the laboratory argument is strikingly hollow. We have no real reason to think that natural scientists can or need to replicate whatever datum is being analyzed. Obviously astronomers cannot reconstruct the life of the solar system; nor do physicists draw all conclusions from laboratory results. At any rate, the question of replication always amounts to the interaction of salient variables, not the construction of a microcosm, and if historians fail in this it is not due to the scope of their phenomena but to the fact that no significant regularities are apparent within these phenomena. Even so, controlled experiments are possible in the social sciences to a limited degree. Much of the work done in small group studies, simulation, computer models, and the like represent attempts to manipulate isolated variables of the larger social system.[11]

This brings us back to the claim of uniqueness. In one sense, the argument holds prima facie; and that is that historical events differ necessarily in terms of time or place, and thus each is by definition unique. The basis for this argument is the assertion that time and place are essential characteristics of historical events, even though they may not be so for natural events. But the question is usually posed another way, which is whether or not events differing in time or place—in varying contexts, that is—can be the same in every other way. This issue can be reduced to whether the variables of history can be located more than once, or whether what occurs is wholly random and new; for if some pattern emerges, then the generalized constructs of natural science are applicable. But if each event is unique, then generalities will be vacuous.

It can be demonstrated that this question, asked in this way, is irrelevant; for no one could seriously deny the uniqueness of specific events. For one thing, too many variables must be accounted for to demonstrate duplication.

[11] For an overview of these approaches, consult the following volumes: Leon Festinger and Daniel Katz, *Research Methods in the Behavioral Sciences* (New York: The Dryden Press, 1953); or, Sidney Ulmer, ed., *Introductory Readings in Political Behavior* (Chicago: Rand, McNally & Co., 1961).

For another thing, there is no real need to deny it. The actual question has never been whether or not historical variables are repeated, but whether or not there exists similarity adequate to establish a general class in órder to subsume historical events under an empirical regularity. A certain amount of tension always obtains between the specific and the general, in the sense that no class concept ever completely incorporates the features of any given unit which it categorizes. But some common properties must prevail to allow for the generality. So the problem in assessing the appropriateness of theoretical schemes for historical phenomena is that of determining what common properties specific historical sequences possess, and to what degree.

Part of the problem is that historical sequences embrace both collective and individual events. Classification of collective events is more difficult because the number of known instances is quite small, and important differences obtain even between those that do occur. The French Revolution may be taken as a recurring type of event: a revolution. But revolutions are both complex and infrequent for purposes of class determination. Moreover, collectivities of this size really cannot be specified into their constituent parts, at least not in any exhaustive sense, which in turn means that they are not observable even in principle. Many collectivities can be observed, such as crowd behavior, but those involving a great many variables cannot be. This means that very large collectivities cannot be classified on an observational basis.[12]

Again, one must be careful not to take this difficulty too far. Few things can be totally observed. The question is whether conclusions about observable events are sufficient as premises for deducing some statement about the characteristics of collectivities. If a collectivity is taken as nothing more than an empirical event, then this inference can be

[12] Nagel, *The Structure of Science* (New York: Harcourt, Brace and World, 1961), pp. 537–606.

made; if not, not. For those who deny any metaphysical existence to a collectivity (over and above its constituent parts), the problem of classification is reduced to deciding when sufficient information is at hand for subsumption under the class in question.

MAX WEBER

The fundamental tension indicated up to now between naturalism and a subjectivist approach to social analysis can be pursued further in the methodological axioms of Max Weber. Weber's significance for methodology is his attempt to pull together many of the disparate (and seemingly contradictory) themes we have identified. This should not be taken to mean that the natural and social sciences merge in Weber, for he maintains that in form they are heterogeneous. But in his own methodology he attempts to combine the necessary dimensions of both. For Weber, cultural data are always specific, yet explanation of any sort entails general laws.

The contradiction apparent in a synthesis of these two stipulations is avoided by separating (once more) method and substance. A law as used here by Weber refers only to a methodological category which meets the logical requirements of strict analysis, and not to a characteristic of the social phenomena being studied. Weber argues strongly and consistently against the reduction of cultural data to any set of laws, especially those which purport to allow reality to be deduced from them. The goal of social science as Weber postulates it is to understand the characteristic uniqueness of the reality in which one exists, and this entails making intelligible both the cultural significance of individual events and the causes of their being so and not otherwise. But such an explanation (in this account) encounters a string of infinite factors, and any attempt to subsume such plenitude under laws is impossible.

The social scientist, in Weber's view, is thus bound by two requirements. First, he must analyze cultural data in terms of their specificity, and not reduce them to any set of laws. This means that explanation must be framed in terms of the unique configurations of social phenomena. No generalized pattern exceeding particular situations is possible without distorting the possibilities of the phenomena. Second, the analyst must construct general conceptual schemes to make the phenomena meaningful. But these constructs do not objectively reflect that which is studied. They are the direct products of the analyst; and without them he cannot make the data intelligible.

The reason for this is basic: Weber holds that all intelligibility comes about because of the activity of the knowing subject. Historical phenomena possess neither common nor dissimilar properties. Any class concept must accordingly be imposed upon them. In fact, the world is presented to the observer chaotically; and whatever meaning it accrues is put there by the conscious agent and is not intrinsic to the phenomena. This entails cutting out a slice of the reality presented. Even a bland description necessitates some narrowing of focus. An explanation involves a more complex limiting of those numberless components constituting a historical event. But this narrowing and limiting is done by the analyst, with nothing in the specific data to guide him. Thus laws are always subjective constructs; and all analysis of cultural phenomena is from a particular point of view.

> The fate of an epoch which has eaten of the tree of knowledge is that it must know that we cannot learn the *meaning* of the world from the results of its analysis, be it ever so perfect; it must rather be in a position to create this meaning itself. It must recognize that general views of life and the universe can never be the products of increasing empirical knowledge . . .[13]

[13] Max Weber, *The Methodology of the Social Sciences*, trans. Edward A. Shils and Henry A. Finch (Glencoe, Ill.: The Free Press, 1949), p. 57.

Meaningfulness does not, for Weber, coincide with laws; and, in fact, the more general the law, the less the coincidence. The specific meaning which a datum possesses for the human observer is not found in those relationships which it might seem to share with other data. It is precisely to the specificity of historical phenomena that the social scientist must turn for understanding. The tension obtaining in any case between the general and the specific now reveals a parallel tension for Weber between the generality of a law and its explanatory power in cultural data: the more general the law, the less valuable it is. This is due to the fact that generality means the absence of content, since the content here is specific cultural data.

In Weber's framework the objective analysis of cultural events is therefore impossible for two fundamental reasons. First, knowledge of social laws is not knowledge of social reality, but at best only a means to attain this end. Second, knowledge of cultural events is inconceivable except on the basis of the significance which the relevant splinters of reality have for us in certain specific situations. The necessary selecting and ordering of phenomena is entirely different from the analysis of reality in terms of laws and general concepts. The conclusion is that all knowledge of cultural reality is always knowledge from particular points of view.

These observations may be taken to mean that, as far as Weber is concerned, no analysis is capable of penetrating the entirety of ontological reality.[13] We always see from a perspective, which is needed to make sense of the world. But this does not invalidate analysis, for Weber also holds that the way in which an object is chosen (or constructed) is a different kind of enterprise than verification of the results of the analysis. There is contingency only in the selective process; once the phenomenon has been isolated (or given

[14] This is Parsons' assertion in his introduction to Max Weber's *The Theory of Social and Economic Organization* (Glencoe, Ill.: The Free Press, 1964), pp. 8–29.

significance), then the standards of science govern the investigator. This is true even though what governs the choice of an object for investigation is far from the mood of science: the evaluative ideas which dominate the investigator and his age.

This acceptance of cultural direction places Weber very much in the empiricist tradition, and of course subjects him to the same problems of relativism discussed earlier. As with Mannheim, Weber wants to view mathematics and logic as universal while allowing for relativity elsewhere. Unlike Mannheim, he comes off fairly well in his arguments. The reason for this is that his claims for science are modest indeed. Weber argues that "a correct scientific proof must be acknowledged as correct even by a Chinese,"[15] but this acknowledgment applies only to the methods of the analysis. The ends of the scientific enterprise are questions of circumstances. The means are universal.

The notion of means as universally valid, however, will not go very far. Weber himself consistently acknowledges that every definition is finally a human one, and so cannot adequately be explained without the fact of cultural influence. This acknowledgment recognizes a fundamental problem in the social sciences, which is the choice of words. Even in simple description one must use language; and the question of appropriate language is a different enterprise than description as such, or (for that matter) any other task for which language is a necessary instrument. But if, as Weber admits, there can be no definitive vocabulary for the analysis of social phenomena, then even the means of science (logic and mathematics, which are of course linguistically based) are culturally relative.

A problem also arises from the status of means. The internal validity of logic and mathematics holds when these systems are viewed in themselves, or independent of their

[15] Weber, *The Methodology of the Social Sciences, op. cit.*, p. 58.

use. But science is activity, which suggests that the means of logic and mathematics must be taken in terms of research goals. This leads to trouble. Objective techniques might be more or less appropriate to given goals; and thus the effectiveness or ultimate correctness of the means by which the analysis is verified becomes a variable of the goal chosen. The immediate objection to this is that the correctness of a proof holds even if the proof is developed or applied incorrectly by specific individuals. But what is involved here is precisely this business of application, for to say (as Weber does) that scientific techniques are universal refers to the *use* of certain methodological principles; and this makes these principles relative to the kinds of tasks for which they are used.

So far Weber does not get the best of it. But science in his terms is itself simply a means, and not an end. This means that final purposes are outside the confines of the scientific enterprise, and, further, that science is a way of looking at the world with no ultimate validity for the enterprise as a whole. Proof always takes place within the scientific framework. Hence when Weber argues universality of techniques he can get away with it by meaning that *if* one were to adopt certain methods, *then* certain conclusions will follow. In these terms, a Chinese may acknowledge the correctness of a scientific proof, but only insofar as he shares the basic features of science. Universality is possible for Weber when it is based on a contingency, which is the affirmation of science in the first place.

This is not so small an achievement as one might at first imagine. To say that scientific proof is always valid for those who are scientists at the very least establishes an orderly system of expectations. No proof, as we have seen, escapes its presuppositions. The affirmation of science may be taken as an acceptance of premises; and that conclusions flow in an orderly fashion from these premises is a conditional but authentic universality. One might object that the whole enterprise of science is culturally relative. Who would deny it? The point is that this begs the question. Scientists do not (for Weber) engage questions that extend beyond the instrumental framework of science, or those requiring ultimate verification. Unlike Ayer, Weber does not claim final validity for science itself. It is universal only in the sense that assuming the scientific framework places one within a common conceptual order.

The Ideal Type

The problem that Weber poses for himself is resolving that friction between objectivity and subjectivity which corresponds to the respective differences between natural science and a more intuitive approach to analysis. Reduced to the kind of themes that have been indicated so far, this entails constructing generalized categories which meet logical requirements and which at the same time embody the point of view peculiar to the historical and cultural sciences: the use of subjective forms. Weber's solution to this problem is to adopt the notion of *ideal type*, which purports to fulfill logical requirements while remaining as close as possible to the concrete individual reality.

The ideal type is a conceptual scheme which is constructed from the point of view of the persons whose action is being studied, although it is assigned to this perspective by the analyst.[16] This concept may vary considerably from that set of actual constructs constituting the analyst's point of view. Even logic and mathematics, Weber concedes, can have a cultural validity for members of a culture which may appear absurd to one studying the culture. Validity in this sense operates on two levels: that intrinsic to the analytic system, or, better, that defined by the analyst; and the way in which this system might be made culturally meaningful.

[16] Max Weber, *Basic Concepts in Sociology*, trans. H. P. Secher (New York: The Citadel Press, 1962), p. 29.

Analytic thought may be either the object of investigation, or the a priori basis of investigation; and hence two standards of correctness exist, one for the actor and one for the analyst.

We must understand this distinction in order to appreciate the fact that the ideal type is a norm conforming completely to neither of these two standards. It *is* a product derived from the actor's point of view, but it embodies the logical ideal of this perspective. We may also say that the ideal is a construct of the analyst; or, as Weber would hold, it is that analytic standard of logic and mathematics which is universal. In this sense, the ideal type is both subjective and objective: it is the way in which an actor would construct his world, or act in it, if he were perfectly rational.

This departs from the attempt in classical philosophy to secure a total knowledge of reality. A part of experience as studied with Weber's system will always remain outside the analytic categories. Nor does it embody any single principle to explain phenomena, as the evolutionary thesis of biology purports to reflect the underlying law of events. The ideal type is always a specific construct for some particular cultural setting. It expresses the characteristic features of a phenomenon, or that which is essential to its being what it is. But it is not in any way an average. Rather, it is formed by the one-sided accentuation of one or more subjective points of view and by the synthesis of a plurality of data into a unified analytic construct.[17]

What must be avoided here is considering the ideal type as an abstraction of the typical. It is not, for this would exclude the accidental features of the datum. The guiding principle in this abstraction is always explanation. The ideal type functions as a methodological instrument to make phenomena meaningful, and can only be judged in terms of its utility in doing this. Whether it really reflects the typical or average is an inappropriate question. Also, as a logical

[17] Weber, *The Methodology of the Social Sciences, op. cit.*

abstraction of actual relationships the ideal type can never be found fully realized anywhere in empirical reality. In this sense, the construct is a utopia, or normative ideal. But the norm envisaged here is a purely rational norm with no prescriptive overtones. The utopia is not one which ought to be realized, but only the logical ideal of a specific cultural field. In this way it is a construct to assess the extent to which reality diverges from the logical norm, but only insofar as this makes the real understandable to the analyst.

Actors may well have within their minds certain normative ideas to which they aspire, either as personal goals or as maxims for the regulation of general social relationships. But this kind of normative ideal is different than the ideal type, even if the same fundamental idea is expressed within the analytic scheme. The reason for this explains the distinction between Weber's ideal and an actual datum: ideas in men's minds are always psychologically and not logically conditioned. This means that they are unavoidably vague. For an actual ideal to be transformed into an ideal type would entail abstracting the essential features of the empirical ideal and shaping them into logical consistency. This, then, as the essence of the phenomenon in question, could function as a conceptual device to make generally intelligible the subjective ideal embraced by people in society. This logical ideal type could accordingly function as a norm to which someone might strive, but in the process of incorporating the logical norm into the personal sphere of meaning, the ideal type would unavoidably be distorted by the subject. Thus, Weber's construct functions *as an ideal type* only in terms of a utopia.

As a utopia it still describes a probable state of affairs, but the probability is an objective one. That is, the ideal type expresses the perfectly rational pattern of a subjective point of view. This means that both ends and means must be constructed by the analyst for the actor, but both must represent the objective essence of the actor's point of view. So the conditions categorized always imperfectly reflect the complete empirical phenomenon, even though people will always diverge to some degree from the conceptual ideal. For the analyst, the ideal type functions as the tool with which to understand the behavior of those who are more subjective than rational. This makes possible the ordering of reality in accord with categorical assumptions which are subjective in a specific sense.

ATTITUDINAL VARIABLES

The task to which Weber addresses himself has been continued in contemporary political analysis. One of the distinctive features of behavioralism is the introduction of an attitudinal variable between sociological data and political behavior.[18] This attitudinal variable is brought into the analytic framework as a means of reconstructing the political system from the viewpoint of the participant, and in this way merging the subjective and objective dimensions of the social world as Weber attempts to do with the ideal type. Put into a more modern terminology, the older stimulus–response model has been replaced by a stimulus–organism–response model.

Hence, the authors of *The American Voter*[19] claim to be doing a "phenomenological" study of the United States political system by virtue of the fact that the perspectives of political actors are treated as causal variables of the first rank. In the conceptual scheme used, the funnel of causality, variables are taken in terms of three dichotomous sets: exogenous–relevant; external–personal; and nonpolitical–political. Relevant variables are defined by the fiat of the

[18] For an elaboration of this, see Charles Osgood, "Behavior Theory and the Social Sciences," in Roland Young, ed., *Approaches to the Study of Politics.*

[19] Angus Campbell *et al.*, *The American Voter* (New York: John Wiley & Sons, 1960).

analyst. But both personal and political variables are defined by the actor, the former as what is within the cognitive field of the actor and the latter as what is taken as political by the actor. Further, the closer one gets in time to the dependent variable, the more relevant, personal, and political the antecedent variables become.[20]

But the success of the subjective–objective synthesis must be weighed against two important considerations. First, only as subjective behavior is rational can it be handled by the political investigator. This means, in the broadest sense, that an actor must behave in a way that is comprehensible in terms of some set of concepts available to the political analyst. Otherwise, obviously, the behavior is not explainable. (On this point, more later.) Second, the viewpoint of an actor contains both conscious and unconscious characteristics, and only the conscious dimension is gotten at with attitudinal variables currently in use.

The classic work in treating the role of the unconscious in political behavior is Harold Lasswell's *Psychopathology and Politics*.[21] The analytic framework adopted by Lasswell is by now both well known and well criticized. Basically, the thesis is that political man is distinguished from his less active colleagues by virtue of the fact that he displaces his private emotions as public objects, and then rationalizes this displacement in terms of public interests. The difficulty with this and all psychoanalytic approaches to political life is that they become bound to the particular version of psychoanalysis which allows the interpretation in question to be made. A different view of psychology would arrive at conclusions considerably different than those advanced in Lasswell's work.

[20] This confuses a time dimension with a salience dimension, but a criticism of this overlap would be peripheral to the main arguments here.

[21] Lasswell, *Psychopathology and Politics* (New York: The Viking Press, 1960).

But, on the other hand, this difficulty is not solely the property of psychoanalytic approaches. The application of one set of concepts or another to the political world yields varying conclusions whatever technique used. Unfortunately, however, too little has been done since Lasswell in the study of unconscious motivation within the political system, even though such work might well produce crucial links between individual orientations and the performance of the political system as a whole.[22] We are left for now, therefore, with the first consideration, rational behavior, as a concept in use which can demonstrate the troubles embodied in any subjective–objective synthesis.

RATIONALITY

The concept "rationality" is rarely treated in consistent fashion, even though it is central to the idea of a social science. Three main uses of the concept can be identified. First, rational behavior may be defined as the optimum conjunction of means and ends; or, given any goal, that behavior which secures the posited goal with the least amount of difficulty is the optimum rationality in the circumstances. Second, rationality may be defined as rule-playing according to some game. Third, rational action may be defined as that behavior based on perfect knowledge. All of these definitions have their special problems, but each is a distinct approach. Part of Weber's problem is a confusion between the first and second uses of rationality.

The means-ends definition of rationality presupposes that evidence can be adduced to demonstrate an appropriate connection of means and ends. Such an assumption is safe enough at the level of a paradigm case. If an individual wants to go west, and proceeds knowingly to the east, then we are justified in saying that he is irrational. What makes this

[22] See Robert Lane's *Political Ideology* (Glencoe, Ill.: The Free Press, 1962) for some mild exceptions to this observation.

a paradigm case is that it is a purely theoretical relationship of inconsistent behavior. The evidence, that is, is a conflict of theoretical categories: desire *west*, knowing pursuit *east*. Means-ends judgments on the factual success of an enterprise rely on such norms of consistency. But these norms cannot be factually established in social inquiry.

One distinction which must be maintained in a means-ends system is that between *rational* and *mistaken* behavior. If an individual wants to go west, and then goes east with the thought that he is going west, we would not want to say that he is acting irrationally. He has simply made an error. The importance of this distinction lies in the additional factors it introduces. To get at truly irrational behavior now entails finding out the level of information of an actor in order to determine whether or not he is acting in accordance with that information. The correct association of means and ends cannot be imposed on the actor by fiat of the analyst.

Ignoring the distinction between irrational and mistaken behavior leads to a gross misinterpretation of a social system. If we say that political actors are not voting their interests because they are irrational, then we are implying that a change in the level of information will not predictably affect their behavior. On the other hand, mistaken behavior is capable of being influenced by changes in information. Hence if we leave out the distinction in question, we misrepresent the possibilities for behavior resulting from the interaction of information and attitudes.

Yet the observance of this distinction presents no less troublesome a problem. By taking account of an actor's information level we become mired in the dilemma of defining irrational behavior from within the actor's frame of reference. The paradigm case of the individual desiring to go west and yet knowingly setting off for the east is almost impossible to establish factually. On what grounds could we infer that west is the real goal when east is the actual goal of the actor's behavior? Aside from the difficulties of unconscious goals, the fact that an individual acts in a certain way is evidence for saying that this behavior defines his real goal. If an individual goes east, then we would ordinarily say (given that the goal is defined by the actor) that we were mistaken in taking his goal to be west.

Take as a concrete example the proclivity of some low-income groups to vote against the graduated income tax. The compelling temptation for the analyst is to attribute irrationality to this behavior. But this can only be done by ignoring the frame of reference of these groups. Within the information level of these individuals such a voting pattern may be wholly rational. The problem suggested here is that all behavior embraced by a means-ends system must be goal-oriented; and since the goals must be defined by the actor, then any behavior can be defined as rational by any actor. Hence we are confronted with the tautology that because an actor does something he is behaving rationally.

Another acute difficulty in means-ends rationality is the status of the goal itself. Consider a situation where an individual decides to carry out what may be considered a thoroughly irrational act. Say he resolves to kill the woman he loves. This being the goal, it is possible in means-ends analysis to assess the rationality of the means he uses to accomplish this purpose; and if he carries out the act with dispatch and a minimum of difficulty, then we might say he has acted rationally in the kind of things he did to secure his goal. But of course the goal is insane; and unless we can evaluate the means in terms of the sensibility of the goal itself, that is, outside the specific means-ends system, then the whole notion of rationality has a nightmarish quality to it. What this suggests is that means-ends analysis confuses the idea of efficiency with that of rationality; and the latter notion seems to entail an open-ended system, or continuing process of evaluation, in order to view any posited goal as also a means to some further end.[23]

[23] Peter Blau, "Critical Remarks on Weber's Theory of Authority," *American Political Science Review*, LVII (June, 1963), pp. 305–16.

One way to get out of these difficulties is to adopt the second definition of rationality, which is rule-playing according to some game. This is the option chosen by Anthony Downs in *An Economic Theory of Democracy*,[24] although he does not affirm the idea of gaming explicitly. Downs focuses on the economic or political goals of an individual. This allows him to bypass the conundrums of accounting for decisions emerging from the total personality of an individual. Rational behavior is defined in terms of a specified system, and nothing else. If an individual purposely loses money on the stock market, he is irrational from the perspective of the stock market, even though this may be perfectly rational behavior in terms of his psychological needs.

A version of the game definition of rationality is often presented as the good-reasons argument associated with modern British empiricism.[25] A man is rational by this account if he has good reasons for doing what he does. If an individual responds to the faulty performance of his automobile by lifting the hood and searching about in the area of the car's sparkplugs and so on, then he is rational on the grounds that a plausible connection exists between the car's performance and the mechanical parts he is investigating. If he were to utter incantations to the moon, then he would be acting irrationally. This is no more or less than a version of game rationality, for muttering to the moon is irrational only within the context of certain cultural rules; and unless we want to buy the dubious notion that some systems of behavior have a firm grip on reality while others do not, we can only attribute rationality on the basis of a system (and not to the systems themselves).

The difficulties in game rationality follow from the examples. First, the system itself cannot be judged as rational

[24] Downs, *An Economic Theory of Democracy* (New York: Harper & Row, 1957).

[25] Quentin Gibson, *The Logic of Social Inquiry* (New York: The Humanities Press, 1959), pp. 156–78.

or irrational. Second, and more significant from an empirical point of view, individuals may be playing more than one game, or a game other than the one in which they appear as formal members. As Downs points out, a man may vote for a candidate just to placate his nagging wife.[26] The man losing money on the stock market may be playing a game of personal masochism. These problems cannot be gotten around. They are part of the game definition of rationality. But they become palatable on the basis of one steadying assumption: in scientific analysis the individual is taken only in terms of an objective system. The subjective discussion of social life, in brief, must be sacrificed to secure empirical laws.

Rationality and Subjectivity

The third definition of rationality, behavior based on perfect knowledge, sharply demonstrates this tension between subjectivity and scientific knowledge. With this use of rationality, the analyst constructs a model of the subjective state which would correspond to the world *if* an actor possessed full insight into both his situation and that of others relevant to the defined activity. This definition is different than the previous two for a single reason: perfect awareness embraces areas outside any means-ends or game system; for in both previous definitions of rationality the universe under consideration has been circumscribed conceptually, while perfect knowledge is without bounds.

The problem with a perfect-knowledge definition of rationality is precisely its antagonism with the actor's viewpoint. It does not, that is, get at what it purports to get at. Subjectivity is of course always less than full cognition, which would amount to omniscience. But to use perfect knowledge even as an ideal model of subjectivity, never fully realized in the world, is impossible. One crucial aspect

[26] *Op. cit.,* p. 7.

of a subjective perspective is the presence of a sense of *here-ness*, or a specific location with which to view the world. The alter ego is defined in part as a consciousness not myself, which I know to be true because I am *here* and the other is *there*. What is more, I experience the other in terms of my own set of typicalities, or what I have come to expect from him. I do not directly experience his subjectivity.

But what will ensue if I have perfect awareness? For one thing, my positional sense of *here* will be lost, for only as I can identify my ego as not the remainder of the world do I have location. That is, I know only my own subjectivity in the commonsense world. But perfect awareness allows me to experience the subjectivity of the other, and the distinction between ego and alter ego is lost. In fact, there is no more "other" as opposed to the self, for perfect awareness means that the self is all consciousness within the reality embraced by the analytic construct. In short, the actor assumes the role of God, or Everyman, within the concept. He is no longer subjective in any sense.

To define rationality as perfect knowledge moves the concept to a category different in *kind* than the subjective orientation it is supposed to represent. Hence it cannot function as an ideal model for the actor's viewpoint, for an ideal model must possess the fundamental categories of that which it represents. In the case of perfect knowledge, what are excluded are the very conditions which make for subjective viewing: the positional character of an actor. This model of rationality therefore does not incorporate the actor's perspective either perfectly or imperfectly.

All definitions of rationality are vulnerable to the same difficulty. If the actor's viewpoint is embodied in the analytic construct, then rational behavior cannot be usefully separated from irrational behavior. But if criteria are introduced to allow the rational–irrational distinction, then the analytic construct gets away from that which it is trying to explain, which is the way in which actors ascribe meaning to what they do. The dilemma of rationality puts into relief the broader problem of science and human behavior; for to the degree that science is objective or universal knowledge, it too is not coincidental with the subjective or specific viewings of actors.

SCIENCE AND SUBJECTIVITY

Subjective viewing is not entirely specific. If it were, then we would have no common experience and therefore no communication. Subjectivity is grounded on the assumption that others do exist and also see the world as, say, I see it; and seeing the world in a common fashion entails shared expectations. These are acquired in the socialization process. No doubt there are periods of social disruption which shatter the traditional social fabric. But we would expect that they merely substitute new sets of expectations for the old, perhaps even terror for security. A social order of any kind entails common orientation for its members.

But the arena of typicalities does not exhaust all there is to subjectivity. An actor's viewpoint is comprised of both the immediate focus of his attention as well as the pluralistic background to this focus. Perception is a constant interaction between that which is the specific subject of viewing and that which is a set of assumptions for the special purpose at hand. Nothing, even at the center of focus, can be seen totally; for the specific location of an individual allows him to see (as Plato realized) only adumbrations of the world. Within the subjective point of view are cognitive, cathectic, and evaluative orientations.[27]

Scientific categories do not fit this general sketch of subjectivity. Instead of a specific location, the scientific observer has no sense of location. Any individual, ideally, should be able to arrive at similar conclusions no matter who he is. This is the fundamental feature of scientific verifica-

[27] For one of the pioneer works in distinguishing these orientations, refer to Talcott Parsons and Edward Shils, eds., *Toward A General Theory of Action* (New York: Harper & Row, 1951), pp. 3–27.

tion. Subjectivity, on the other hand, is entirely a matter of *who* is observing, for each individual is distinct from every other (even though certain typicalities are shared) by virtue of his factual existence. Further, only the cognitive mode of orientation is adopted in science, while affective orientations form an important area of subjectivity. These affective orientations include what may be considered irrational factors from the perspective of scientific norms.

But surely, one may argue, science takes account of specific or irrational factors. What is Weber's ideal type but the conceptualization of subjectivity? A social science (the argument might continue) incorporates subjective factors as part of an objective construct, which is necessary for purposes of validation. The *construct* is general and objective, but it includes *subjective* factors. But this objection misses the point. The social event can be conceptualized, but not in the real sense of its occurrence. As it occurs it is subjective, for it means nothing except as it is given meaning by those within the event. This meaning, in turn, must be reconstructed by the analyst in general form. It is the general dimension of the event which science handles. The residue of specificity which goes into marking the distinction between objective and subjective knowledge remains behind.[28]

This general antagonism between science and subjectivity would hardly bother Weber, who is at great pains to demonstrate precisely this. But the problems indicated here come home to plague his methodology as he tries to bring together these two disparate areas, for they will not fit. If the results of analysis are to be scientifically valid, then they must assume an objective form. Otherwise they are personal conclusions. These requirements do not paralyze social inquiry, for no analyst purports seriously to reflect all of social reality

[28] Michael Polanyi develops a similar distinction between scientific and ordinary perception in terms of a unity principle. He claims that scientists perceive *gestalten* which indicate a true coherence in nature. Ordinary perception does not discern this coherence. See "The Logic of Tacit Inference," in *Philosophy* (January, 1966), pp. 1–18.

in his theory (least of all Weber). But they do indicate a problem for the social sciences which does not hold for the natural sciences; nor is it solved by the introduction of ideal types.

Explanation in the Ideal Type

Does the ideal type explain? Or does it need to? The answer to the second question is an obvious yes, if we mean that the concept has to reveal something about the social world in the way of public knowledge. (Otherwise it cannot be justified as an analytic device.) But the first question is more difficult. Certainly the ideal type does not explain if we take explanation to mean subsumption under a universal or statistical regularity, for Weber is directing his methodology away from the natural sciences.

But we should not be seduced into thinking that explanation ends where science does unless we have good reasons for doing so. A distinction between explanation and understanding is helpful. The former term is usually taken as an act making plain or intelligible what is not so plain or intelligible. To understand means to grasp the meaning of something. What is important here is that one can personally understand without explanation; or, to reverse the emphasis, explanation entails *conveying* understanding to others.

This small difference outlines the answer. To explain a social event (as we have seen) means that one has translated it into symbols which can be shared by others; or, one has generalized it in some fashion. The understanding Weber wants to convey is specific and subjective. In its primitive state, therefore, it cannot be conveyed to others. To explain the datum in question necessitates altering it. This antagonism, of course, may be drawn too severely. The same social event, *generally* taken, emerges in the form of public knowledge, and hence the ideal type possesses explanatory power. But some residue of meaning always remains outside an explanatory construct, for the general properties of an event do not exhaust all of its properties. What holds true for science generally also applies to the ideal type: publicly verified knowledge is not social reality.

Explanation and Prediction

The conclusion to be drawn at this stage of the discourse is not that there cannot be a science of social phenomena. There can be, but only at a certain price. The price is the sacrifice of the distinctiveness of social events. Science is concerned with establishing causal relations and general laws. To do this the social scientist must concentrate on systematic patterns of human conduct. Only as an event is a recurring instance of a general class can it be treated scientifically. Again, this does not exclude entirely the subjective meanings of actors. But it includes these meanings only as they can be translated into objective or general terms.

It follows that the primary usefulness of science in scrutinizing cultural events is in the area of established behavior patterns. This observation is borne out in political analysis, where the most striking successes of scientific investigation have been in the area of voting behavior. An election is held at systematic intervals. Further, voters (at least in the United States) cast their ballots with a fairly high degree of consistency from one election to another.[29] To the degree that such behavior is systematic it is amenable to the techniques of science. The behavior, that is, can be generalized and placed within empirical regularities.

One word of caution. To say that social phenomena are amenable to empirical regularities is not equivalent to the proposition that they have been explained. An event of the physical world is explained by doing this, because it has no subjective dimensions. Once we have adequately accounted for the external movements of a star, we have done all that we can do. But social events must be treated from the inside.

[29] Campbell *et al.*, *op. cit.*, *The American Voter*. See especially the importance of party identification as a stabilizing factor.

Hence the establishment of systematic patterns of behavior must be supplemented with the subjective meanings of actors, even though these meanings must be reconstructed away from the *Lebenswelt* as scientific constructs.

This cautionary note also suggests that prediction is not equivalent to explanation. We can, for example, subsume the ebb and flow of the tides under some pattern of numbers that will allow us to predict accurately when the ocean will be in or out. Yet this is not an explanation. It is only a correspondence between the tides and our numerical system. Conversely, an explanatory theory may be quite poor as a tool for predictions. Darwin's theory of evolution is an example.[30] These observations apply with even greater forcefulness to social inquiry, where the commonsense explanations of actors must be taken into account.

A statistical correlation, therefore, is not in itself an explanation, although it may function as a tool to make predictions. We have seen (cf. Chapter III) that even if sunspots were perfectly correlated with business cycles, we would not normally offer this correlation as an explanation of business cycles. The reason for this is to be found in our general view of the world: no plausible connection exists between sunspots and business cycles. The requirement, then, that must be satisfied in any explanation is that the explanatory framework account for the facts in a way that is consistent with our general *Weltanschauung*, or paradigm. This requirement extends over both the physical and social sciences.

The condition which makes explanation possible—a conceptual framework—is itself of social origin. Aristotle's assertion that man is a social animal has been adequately substantiated; we cannot imagine an individual developing a language in complete isolation from other men. Therefore, it is from our common experience that the possibilities for explaining the world derive, for without a social world no

[30] Stephen Toulmin, *Foresight and Understanding* (New York: Harper & Row, 1963), pp. 18–43.

language would exist, and hence no paradigm would exist. For the social sciences this means that what is being explained—society—is itself the necessary condition for social inquiry.

Further, inasmuch as the social event *is* a social event only from the perspective of the participants, it is also necessary for the social analyst to share that mental framework assumed by the participants the analyst studies. This is what makes all social inquiry a conceptual as well as an empirical task.

> Historical explanation is not the application of generalizations and theories to particular instances: it is the tracing of internal relations. It is like applying one's knowledge of a language in order to understand a conversation rather than like applying one's knowledge of the laws of mechanics to understand the workings of a watch.[31]

But, like the physical scientist, the social analyst must also convey his knowledge in the form of publicly validated conclusions. It is not enough to understand the conversation; one must also communicate this understanding to others. Otherwise there exists no such thing as social inquiry. Unfortunately, the translation of subjective meaning to general symbols alters that meaning. This is the fundamental tension in all social investigation: the analyst must be both observer and participant, the one to build a body of accessible knowledge, the other to know what is happening.

THE VALIDATION OF SCIENCE

It remains to be seen how we decide whether the price of science is a bargain or not. Science itself will not tell us one way or another. It is, as we have seen, a way of looking at the world which yields publicly validated knowledge. But as

[31] Peter Winch, *The Idea of a Social Science* (New York: Humanities Press, 1958), p. 133.

a means to secure such knowledge it is not self-validating: the scientific enterprise cannot be verified with the scientific method. This means that the general perspective within which scientific research takes place is a commitment prior to science itself. The perennial regress of *why* questions found in all inquiry leads quickly to areas of value choices outside of science.

The areas outside of science, further, are more than prior to science. As a method, science entails a goal or purpose. To define an activity as a means necessitates that it be related to an end; for to say of a method that it has no purpose is an absurdity. The obvious goal of science is to explain experience. But, as we have seen, explanation is an account of the world which allows us to find our way about in it. Part of the game of finding our way about is making choices between alternative courses of action. Therefore the line dividing the explanation of experience (science) from the application of these explanations to change experience (policy) is very thin; and it is in the latter area that value choices again occur.

The picture of science which emerges from this discussion is one of an activity housed between two affirmations. Prior to science is the choice of the scientific perspective. Subsequent to science is policy-making. Between these two areas where value choices must take place is the neutral method aimed at securing verified knowledge. Whether even this circumscribed activity can be neutral in practice remains to be discussed. But values envelop science, even though they may not be a part of the narrow techniques of science; for values are the necessary grounds which make all of science possible.

CHAPTER V

Facts and Values

THE BASIC QUESTIONS

Where values are to be located in political analysis, or if they are to be present at all, has been a subject of dispute at least since the 18th century. The modern thesis on methodological neutrality goes back to Hume, who held that it is impossible to derive a normative statement from any set of statements not including a value premise. Even this, however, was not intended as a complete separation between fact and value, for Hume claimed that the kind of evaluation one makes about an object is related to its factual properties. The relationship simply cannot be construed as a logical one.

This logical separation between facts and values was extended by the earlier positivists to the area of verification. We will recall that in the positivist framework the validity of an empirical statement is determined by the facts of experience, while the validity of an analytic statement depends solely on the definitions of the symbols it contains. Value statements, however, are not (in this intellectual framework) amenable to either empirical or analytic verification. This singular status of value judgments leads to the emotivist position on values, which is the thesis that values are nothing more than emotional expressions with no truth content beyond personal preference.

The positivist thesis on value in social analysis can be traced back to Max Weber. Weber argued that the social scientist cannot *qua* scientist do anything more than describe and explain cultural phenomena. To evaluate the social world normatively is not scientifically possible. Weber's thesis is based on a linguistic distinction between value propositions, and those of analytic or empirical form. One could not sensibly argue that the validation of research conclusions is a factual affair unless the assumption is made that factual statements and value statements *are* different kinds of things. But more than a linguistic distinction comes out of Weber's argument, for what he is suggesting is that this distinction can be reflected in the postures assumed by social analysts. The scientist, that is, can make judgments *in research* which are factual and analytic, but not normative. Hence the issue is one of attitudes, even though a certain linguistic framework is presupposed.

The classical thesis on value differs considerably from the modern set of assumptions. The pre-positivist claim, often called naturalism, is that value statements make truth claims which *can* be factually validated. If, that is, we say that X is good, we are asserting a property of X which can be proved true or false. The evidence adduced to verify this truth claim is, in the naturalistic framework, often some kind of psychological evidence, such as whether the X in question gives us pleasure, delight, and so forth. Psychological naturalism is the most typical form of naturalism, although other positions have been advanced. A common alternative to the psychological version is verification based on whether or not a thing is beneficial to mankind.

These two antagonistic approaches to value can be framed in terms of in-object v. in-subject language. The naturalistic assumption is that goodness is a property of the object which is judged as good. The subjective approach found in positivism defines value judgments as reports on the feelings of the speaker (at best) or mere exhortations which are not really statements at all (at worst). The difficulties with both positions are by now well known. The naturalist is burdened (as we shall see) with the peculiar nature of values which seems to separate them from other ordinary factual properties. Both versions of the positivist approach, on the other hand, lead to the absurdity that one choice is as good as another.

It is the positivist thesis on value which is assumed in contemporary political analysis. This amounts in actual research to a focus on the factual political system to the exclusion of the way it ought to be,[1] which is consistent with what Max Weber posed as the legitimate task for social research. The rationale for excluding values from modern political analysis derives from two common theses of all empirical frameworks: first, that facts and values are conceptually distinct; second, that values cannot be factually validated. These are crucial assumptions for political analysis, for if values are not distinct from facts, then the political investigator cannot conduct value-free research.[2] Further, if values can be factually verified, then the political analyst may legitimately pursue normative research while remaining an empiricist.

On the basis of these preliminary observations it is clear that a large part of the discussion of values in political inquiry must be conducted at the level of meta-ethics, which means engaging questions of definition and verification. This discussion can, in turn, be broken down into three

[1] For the last word on positivist political science, see Arnold Brecht's *Political Theory* (Princeton: Princeton University Press, 1959).

[2] So Leo Strauss argues in *Natural Right and History* (Chicago: University of Chicago Press, 1953).

areas: first, the exact nature of the empiricist distinction between facts and values; second, the possibility of suspending values in empirical research; third, whether the political investigator can make recommendations in the area of policy-making which have some general validity. These areas naturally overlap, for all are closely related to the initial question of how we draw the distinction between facts and values. But taking them separately helps to clear up much of the confusion surrounding the subject of values and politics.

THE FACT-VALUE DISTINCTION

One difficulty contained in any analysis of value is the presence of several different kinds of value judgments. A common separation is that between *ought* judgments and those containing or implying *good* and, a further distinction, *right*. The reasons for this separation are clear enough. "Ought" seems to suggest a primitive norm directing future conduct, as in, "I ought to keep my promises." "Right," on the other hand, refers to an actual or theoretically completed act which is in accord with some more basic norm: "Law X is right," meaning that it is congruent with norm Y. Further, "ought" suggests choice or action, while "good" is more passive. To assert that I ought to do X still leaves open the possibility that I will not do it, while a similar kind of latitude is missing in instances of the goodness of X. That is, X may still not be good, but only if the situation or perceiving subject changes.

The same kind of general analysis can be extended directly to the term "good." When one says that it is good to do something, one is obviously not saying that you or I ought to do it. This claim may not be as compelling in the case of "it is good to *be* X," but at any rate to say that it is good to *do* something (say, exercise in the morning) is not equivalent to saying that one ought to do it (even though the goodness may function as a reason for doing it). Nor, at the same time, is it the same thing as saying that it is "right" to exercise in the morning.

These are only the most general kinds of comments, all of which can be seriously qualified or elaborated. But, in order to get on with the business of evaluating the fact–value distinction, we may move on to a lengthier consideration of only one of these terms: the good. Two uses of *good* are immediately apparent. The first is the predicative use, as, "X is good." The second is the attributive use, as, "X is a good Y." The predicative use of good differs in regard to its object. To say that spinach is good is one thing. To say that Picasso is good is quite another; and while it is true that the predicate *good* is appropriate in both cases, there is an undeniable disparity in elegance between spinach and Picasso, regardless of one's culinary or artistic tastes. This brings up yet another kind of difference: that between questions of taste and ethical judgments. A good Picasso may engender noble sentiments, but it still remains distinct from axioms such as, "To prevent needless suffering is good."

The attributive use of *good* lends itself to similar treatment, but in addition there are meanings peculiar to this use of good which do not emerge from the basic "X is good" model. Where X is good-of-its-kind, it can mean an objective desired by the person so characterized, as, a good thief (although a person may always be judged good on grounds incidental to his desires); or it can mean an expectation of the judging subject, as, a good drink; or it can suggest a stipulated norm, as, a good painting. All of these are what good-of-its-kind ought to be, and can be distinguished from what is typical of its kind, as, a good oak leaf. No doubt these categories overlap, but this is no matter at the moment. These are merely preliminary considerations which bear mentioning before moving on to the main thesis.

One more distinction will complete this opening task, and that is the difference between good-in-itself, and good in terms of consequences. Certainly something can be both

good-in-itself and consequently good, but these two characteristics can in themselves be suitably separated. Exercise
may be a neutral, even a painful, undertaking, and yet be
beneficial because it is conducive to health. In the case of
an aesthetic experience, the goodness of the experience
can outweigh whatever consequential benefits it produces.
Nothing, of course, can be taken solely in terms of good-
in-itself, for even an aesthetic experience can be evalu-
ated in terms of its relaxing effect on the individual experi-
encing it. But, on the other hand, we cannot do away with
the notion of good-in-itself, for there is surely a residue of
goodness in acts like listening to music which cannot be
reduced to consequences alone. Hence, while things may be
difficult to classify as one or the other, their in-themselves
and resultant characters may still be distinguished.

But the main interest at the moment is whether or not
good differs from other properties of an object. It does not,
upon ordinary inspection, seem to be a fact about a thing, or
certainly not an ordinary kind of fact. This can be demonstrated at the very beginning with a few examples. If two
things, X and Y, are alike in every respect, then it does not
seem possible that one could be good and the other not, at
least as we mean intrinsic goodness. Yet it is possible for X
and Y to be alike in every other respect except that X is yellow and Y is not. It is not, by the way, accidental that the
word "seem" is used here, for it will be demonstrated later
that this is only an apparent, and not a real, difference.

One more example is appropriate here. If object X is
intrinsically good at one time, and it does not change in its
other qualities, then it seems as if X must be equally good
at a later time. Again, this does not hold for the property of
yellow, or other similar factual states of X.[3] What appears
to be demonstrated here is that goodness is not a natural

[3] Both these examples are adapted from the arguments of G. E.
Moore, "The Conception of Intrinsic Value," *Philosophical Studies*
(London: Routledge and Kegan Paul Ltd., 1922), pp. 253–75.

feature of a thing. Much, of course, can be made of this, and has been; but for our purposes it is enough to see that a straightforward argument can be constructed which makes goodness seem different from any other property which a thing possesses, and which accordingly seems to make the analysis of a thing's goodness or badness a different enterprise from analysis of its other properties.

On the face of it, this is a modest enough claim. We have seen that strong arguments have been constructed which reveal an even more general separation between facts and values. No one seriously carries this separation forward to a complete distinction, which would be the absurd conclusion that there is no relationship at all between facts and values. Obviously the facts about an object have some bearing on whether it is good or not. But no logical relationship seems to hold between the two. This commonplace difference between the goodness of an object and its factual properties can be explained by a subjective–objective dualism, which is that facts are parts of object language and values remain within subject language.[4]

In opposition to this, and as a way of getting at the distinction which seems to hold in ordinary language between, say, "X is good" and "X is yellow," the suggestion here is that an important similarity holds between facts and values; and while this similarity does not collapse the distinction entirely, it does deny the objective–subjective duality sometimes posited as a parallel to the fact–value dichotomy. What will be proposed is that both facts and values are lodged within subject language, and that what we apprehend in the way of object-properties is not an intrinsic part of these objects.

Certainly *this* is by no means a modest claim. But its reasonableness is easily demonstrated. A fact, after all, is

[4] So Hume tried to do, but with some inconsistencies, in *An Inquiry Concerning the Principles of Morals*. (New York: The Liberal Arts Press, 1957).

nothing more than the subsumption of certain sense-data under a term. When we refer to an object as, say, a chair, all that we are doing is agreeing (tacitly, to be sure) that the cluster of data constituting that kind of object is to be called a chair. This need not open the door to those tedious conundrums coming out of sense-data versus physical-object language, for the whole business of a real world behind what we perceive is not here in question. Whatever we encounter in experience does not affect the fact that these things are designated by terms. So while the expression sense-data may be used to refer to these encounters, it is not meant as a referent to some reality behind the perceiving subject's surroundings.

Nor need we get into the morass of a real or unreal separation between subject and object, which can be framed in terms of whether or not we perceive anything at all except little bits of our own mind. Whether we apprehend our own projections or an external world (of whatever composition), we still grapple with *something*. What is important is that we still encounter this something from within a conceptual scheme of some sort. That is, we see whatever we see from a mental perspective which furnishes meaning to our perceptions. The thing-in-itself is thus fugitive to the observer whether it really exists or not.

The conceptual scheme is salient here, not what it conditions, for conceptual screening suggests that whatever properties an object has are derivative of the mental framework of the subject. Let us consider for a moment an odd situation. Suppose the world existed without any human beings; or, for the sake of precision, without any perceiving subjects. Naturally, this is open to the objection that suppositions of this sort are self-defeating, for imagining such a world automatically injects a perceiving subject into it. But one doesn't have to think of the trees and rivers and so forth to make this example go; all that we need do is admit that this is an existentially possible state of affairs, and then imagine what such a situation would mean in terms of empirical properties.

This is the point at which a qualified sense-data process must be introduced to explain perception; for before we can answer the question of what a world would be like without anyone to perceive it, we must establish what goes on in perception itself. Clearly, we perceive something other than the source of sensory data. This has been an established truth at least since the speed of light was recognized, for the idea that light does have speed means that there is an interval between the existence of an object and seeing it. So a star can cease to exist, and we might still perceive it for thousands of years before becoming aware that it is no longer around.

Again, this does not mean that physical objects need exist behind the data of experience, although it does make the general version of representative perception more plausible. But we may still argue that behind the data in question more data exist, and so forth, which leads to a world without substance and consisting only of the senses and what they interact with. No matter. The point is that we have access to sense-data only, and not anything else. This means that a property like "yellow" is nothing more than certain light waves of special length and texture. Notice that this doesn't suggest that we *mean* these light waves when we use the term yellow, for obviously the experience of apprehending yellow was a real one long before light waves were discovered. But neither does it close out the argument that people were also perceiving these light waves whether they were aware of this or not.

What is being got at here is that a world without perceiving subjects would be a world only of unordered data. This is, admittedly, a hard saying, but no other conclusion can be drawn from a perceptual process which grasps representations and not objects, as demonstrated in the instance of light traveling through space. Further, we cannot ascribe properties to a world of this sort, for we have no way of separating out different kinds of characteristics. What we have is only a myriad of light and sound waves, and so forth, with no ordering principle to make then meaningful. Human beings, after all, apprehend their world only from within circumscribed boundaries established by the limits of the senses. We see only certain areas on a color band and hear only certain frequencies, and the like. It is from within these boundaries that properties are defined. Without this human principle, the order constituting properties would not exist. Things would not be yellow or red or noisy, or even necessarily exist at all.

Thus a fact is nothing more than the structuring of reality by the perceiving subject.[5] It is not something objectively out there to be confronted and recognized. Let's go back to the example of a chair. As indicated, what makes this cluster of data a *chair* is a shared attitude that this term will identify it; and what makes a chair *yellow* is a consensus that this sort of sense-data will be understood as yellow. But, *to a point*, this same process is carried on with the value-term "good." That is, what makes a chair *good* is nothing more than an agreement that certain clusters of data will be viewed as good. In this limited sense, both facts and values are subjective constructs referring to sense-data.

Two important qualifications can be made to this similarity. The first is that considerably less agreement exists on what is to count as good than on what is to count as, say, yellow; and that this is a crucial difference between factual and value matters. This is true, but the disparity of agreement can be explained by the social implications that these two kinds of statements have, and not by any difference in form between a factual and a value determination. Little

[5] This is claimed also (but with different arguments) by a host of others, including David Easton, *The Political System* (Chicago: University of Chicago Press, 1959), p. 53.

importance is attached to the determination that a chair is yellow, while the subsumption of certain sense-data under the broad concept *good* chair means that people will have reasons to act in certain ways toward these kinds of chairs, and so on. Hence the problems involved in agreeing on what is to count as good are not a reason to think that one is necessarily doing something conceptually different in settling on value-properties as opposed to factual-properties.

The second qualification is more serious, and it goes something like this. The predicate *good* can be applied to numerous data-clusters, and what makes a chair good is obviously not what makes a wine good. Yet there are yellow chairs and (let us suppose) yellow wine, and being yellow amounts to the same thing in each instance. True enough. In fact, this begins to get at what is peculiar about the term good. This quality of general applicability has engendered the thought (beginning with Plato) that things which are good possess some common feature by which they may be categorized as good; and, also, that this general feature may be abstracted as the essence of goodness. We have rejected the first part of this by rejecting any intrinsic properties to things; but general applicability is still a characteristic of good, in the sense that it can refer to quite different sorts of things.

What, then, makes good different in this way from a term like yellow? One more example may help. If two people, A and B, have the same fundamental experience, say observing Lincoln's Tomb, we would think it odd if one were to say that the structure is made entirely of stone and the other conclude that it is made entirely of wood. So too would it be unusual if one were to claim that the same building is white and the other swear that it is black. This means, of course, that the apparatus (however it might be constituted) for perceiving these kinds of properties is fairly stable from one person to another, making our experience of sense-data a common one (which is indicated by the greater agreement on colors and the like than agreement on a thing's goodness). But considerably more than this is at stake in value judgments, for two people can view the same building, and yet it would not be at all unusual for A to say that the building is badly put together, and B to say that it is a good building in every respect. Surely something more is involved than a confrontation and labeling of the world.

What is involved is basic enough: a value term represents a positive or negative response by the perceiving subject. This is not to deny the presence of responses in the function of factual terms, for no term is entirely stripped of symbolic or direct emotive significance. In a green world, the property yellow might denote acute terror or delight. But precisely this matter of responses is designated by terms such as good and bad; for value terms do not result in emotion— they *mean* emotion. To say of a wine that it is good means that one *likes* it; and this fundamental notion distinguishes a value from a fact and explains the general applicability of good.

Hence, to say that X is good means that X evokes a favorable response from me, or the person in acquaintance with X, as long, that is, as we realize that X really does not have any properties apart from the perceiving subject. What makes X good *is* the favorable response, not some characteristic which it possesses on its own; put another way, without the acquaintance part we could not meaningfully say that X is good.[6] However, we must be careful not to lean entirely toward the subjective side, for the response denotes an interaction between the person in question and something else. It is simply that the goodness of the something else is reckoned by the perceiving subject, and cannot exist without this subject.

[6] This represents a modification of points made by John Dewey in "The Construction of Good," *Readings in Ethical Theory*, Wilfred Sellars and John Hospers, eds. (New York: Appleton-Century-Crofts, Inc., 1952), pp. 272–91, and also by W. D. Falk in lectures and conversations.

Several things follow from this. The main one is probably that this is, unavoidably, a relativistic position. Since an object is good or bad by virtue of subjective response, then the same object can be either good or bad under varying conditions and with different persons encountering it. This means that two of the situations constructed earlier do not hold. The first of these, we will recall, is that if two objects are alike in every respect, then one cannot be good and the other bad (as can be true about other properties like yellow). But, if our analysis is sound, good and bad can be ascribed not only to identical objects, but also to the same object. In similar fashion, the second example used previously also falls through: that if an object is good at one time and does not change at all, then it must be equally good at a later time. Again, this is false if all that we have developed up to now is true, for different situations and different subjects may obviously change an object's goodness even though it has remained the same in every possible detail. We must conclude, therefore, that the notion of *intrinsic* goodness is not a meaningful concept within an empiricist epistemology.

VALUE STANDARDS

The point to be made forcefully is that these conclusions are applicable only within an empiricist approach. If we move from the assumption that extraexperiential knowledge exists, then properties may be assigned to objects on a nonobservable basis. The Platonic Good is an intuitive truth which does not depend upon sense experience. This does not affect the distinction established here between facts and values, or its relevance to the methodological axioms of modern political inquiry, for it is as an empirical undertaking that a value-free science must be scrutinized. The intuitive alternative to empiricism becomes salient where classical and modern approaches confront the same crucial problem in all value judgments: the question of standards.

The necessity of standards for determining what is actually of value can be demonstrated easily enough with the argument we have been pursuing. The favorable-response model delineated here to explain how facts are distinguished from values has one difficulty of singular concern built into it: distinguishing the good from what *seems* to be good. This distinction opens up a number of dimensions, some of which constitute separate problems (like the difference between what is good and what is pleasurable), but the difference between apparent and real goodness is more important than any other at this point in the analysis. The reason for this is that the distinction in question splits the good from the favorable-response explanation, since what evokes favor may not be good in some other senses, as in terms of the health of the respondent, or his economic status, and so forth.

Perhaps a tired example will sharpen the focus on this problem. Subject A thinks that testing atomic bombs is good, or, to be specific, that atomic testing by his country is good. This means that his acquaintance with atom bomb tests has evoked a favorable response from A, perhaps because the thought of explosions has stimulated him, but more likely because he believes that such testing will lead to a reliable defense system, and the like. Let us say, though, that the testing of atomic bombs by A's country is poisoning the atmosphere, and in fact is slowly destroying the entire world, beginning with A's neighborhood. No one would say that bomb testing of this sort is good, least of all A. Yet he does. A has, in short, made a mistake. Atomic testing is *not* good, even though he thinks it is.

What has been demonstrated by A's mistake is the flaw in any emotivist thesis on values: liking is not equivalent to goodness. This means that while values are separated from facts in an empirical framework on the basis of the responses of the perceiving subject, something more than these responses is needed to make sense of value judgments. This something more is needed even if value judgments are denied general validity; for even as personal responses to experience, the purely emotive rationale is inadequate to account for value. Favorable responses can be as bad for the respondent as for others when they are mistaken, or irrational.

A standard response to this line of argument involves inserting the word *knowledgeable* as a qualification for acquaintance. The advantage of this is clear: the apparent good can only be the result of ignorance. Once one is knowledgeably acquainted with an activity or object, then only the real good (or real bad) will be ascribed. In the case of subject A, knowledgeable acquaintance with the atomic testing would have evoked an unfavorable response, for it would have entailed acquaintance with the atmospheric results. So the problem is solved, for the good is that which evokes a favorable response when the response is grounded in correct knowledge.

This argument is sound, but not really so simple. Let's consider the qualification in a little more detail. In the argument, knowledgeable acquaintance is a necessary condition for determining goodness. This leads immediately to two difficulties. First, one can never be as sure that one is knowledgeable about an object as one can that one is favorably disposed to it. It is, after all, a clear (if not always uncomplicated) matter to like or to dislike a thing; but to *know* it involves one in what seems to be an endless task: weight, size, composition, function, effects, and so on. Complete empirical knowledge about a thing is impossible. This means that the introduction of this qualification creates an uncertainty about goodness which was not present before. It also leads to the problem of defining knowledgeable acquaintance, but we will get to that in a moment.

Second, this qualification, at least in the example used, opens up once more the objective–subjective dualism that has shaped the discussion since the beginning of this book. In the empirical analysis of goodness we have demonstrated the subjectivity of both facts and values, which means that knowledge is always lodged within a point of view in any case. This does not mean that knowledge is personal, but it does mean that general validity refers to shared perspectives and not contact with an objective referent. In the case of the atomic testing, however, a standard of correctness holds which may not be coincidental with any point of view. *Everyone* could be ignorant about the atmospheric results, and hence be in error about the value of testing atomic bombs. This suggests a standard for goodness which may reside outside the subjective boundaries of the responding subject.

Both these immediate observations point to one problem: ascertaining knowledgeable acquaintance. In terms of the first observation, one must stipulate what degree of knowledge is to count as adequate, what not. In terms of the second observation, one must grapple with the source of standards (whether within or outside of the prevailing points of view) which determine adequacy. These are old problems, and lead us back once more to the empiricist–rationalist dialogue. For rationalism, standards exist which are independent of human perspectives. This is the position of classical political philosophy. For empirical inquiry, criteria for certainty must be lodged within human experience.

Each approach has its liabilities. What these are is by now clear. Standards which are independent of human awareness are, by ordinary standards of definition, simply unknowable. Hence, intuitive methods must be introduced. Norms, on the other hand, which are wholly dependent on experience must always be uncertain. But this brief allusion to the twin liabilities of mysticism and error is not meant as a guidepost to selecting one epistemology or another. For one thing, most discourse does not *explicitly* involve epistemological questions, and so many commonsense judgments do not directly engage these liabilities. For another thing, as we have seen, the question of why one accepts a philosophical framework must always be open, for even the most basic claims about knowledge are amenable to queries of validity, and so must be simply affirmed without formal proof.

But epistemological questions begin to emerge whenever ordinary discourse is pushed, or made to come to terms with itself. It is, after all, at a reflective level that we pose the question of how we know what we do know. Hence all social inquiry, as a reflection on the ordinary categories of meaning constructed by actors, must grapple with epistemology; for social theory is *not* ordinary discourse, but is a secondary reconstruction of actor symbols. Further, while epistemologies cannot be defended as systems, it is possible to delineate the kinds of moves that are permissible in various epistemological systems. In this way the limitations and possibilities of different sets of assumptions are made overt.

For better or worse, the prevailing *Weltanschauung* in contemporary political science is empiricism. Therefore the temptation hovering on the periphery of the bomb example, which is to introduce the unknown factor (in this case, the atmospheric results) as an objective standard to ground value judgments, must be ignored. Objectivity in an empiricist framework is not congruence with an independent reference, but the juxtaposition of agreed viewpoints. The distinction between "this *is* X," and "this *seems* to be X" is not that between objectivity and subjectivity. When we say "this *is* X," we mean that in normal conditions any unbiased observer will come to the same conclusion. "This *seems* to be X" means that these stipulations have not been fulfilled. Empirical statements are always probable to the degree that conclusions of public validation are appropriate. Regardless of the pungent consequences, factual knowledge is a variable and not a constant.

The intuitive alternative avoids the problem of error, but (as we have seen) at a price. Grasping a truth independent of experience moves the source of standards to an area outside intellectual discourse. Hence there is little to be said about these standards one way or the other. This observation is not the final word on the intuitive alternative, for the emotivist content of intuitionism gives it a share in the positivist thesis that all value judgments are emotive preferences. Further, the tacit dimension in all epistemologies is a kind of intuitive affirmation. We are all, in this fashion, grounded in noncognitive foundations.

THE VALUE OF VALUE

But the reconstruction of intuitionism will have to wait until classical and modern political inquiry are brought to bear upon one another. Still other questions have more immediacy. To lodge "X is good" with human response recalls the specter of utilitarianism, and, of course, the classic criticism made by value theorists ever since then (mentioned in Chapter III). It is this: when we say that the good is the satisfaction of either human desire or human need, a hidden value premise plagues our argument. This is the premise that it is good to satisfy human desires or needs. Or, put another way, it is not a contradiction to say, for example, that something causes the greatest happiness but it is *not* good. This kind of critique can be made to apply to any definition of good, for we may always meaningfully ask, is X (as a definition of good) itself good?

But there are also severe limitations to this kind of criticism within an empiricist epistemology. A fact, as indicated earlier, is a case of public validation (whether tacit or overt). We may imagine, then, a situation where everyone affirms that X is good, meaning in our analysis that X is deserving of favor or approval. It is quite clear that to assert the contrary, that X is *not* good, would entail reliance on a standard which is independent of public validation, which is impossible in an empiricist framework. The issue here is what is to count as adequate grounds for a judgment; and when one assumes an epistemology which takes truth as a matter of human consensus, then it is impossible to get outside of this consensus without a contradiction.

The confusion over whether what we say is good *is* really good comes about, once more, from the possibility of error. When we concur that X is good, we may still be mistaken. But the ground for determining such a mistake is precisely the same process of concurrence that yields the initial judgment that X is good. In the case of defining the good, therefore, any definition which represents public validation (however difficult this may be to secure in actual circumstances) has reason to be taken as good, for denial can only allude to the possibility of error and not to a standard independent of human concurrence. It must be emphasized, of course, that the reliance, in this discussion, on human response is not equivalent to utilitarianism, but a statement of the parameters enclosing any empirical definition of good.

Finally, any value position may be pursued back to a value premise which cannot be validated by the system of proof presupposed in the initial value judgment. This point has been amply demonstrated in the means-ends arguments of political analysis, where the ultimate or final norm is a predicative good which is simply affirmed but not proved.[7] But a regress of this sort is not confined simply to value judgments. Rather it reveals a feature which is shared by all judgments, whether factual or value. Adducing reasons for any claim assumes a theoretical system which provides criteria for validity; and any system must be assumed without ultimate or final proof.

Several examples from scientific explanation can demonstrate this point. To ask, say, whether a stick which looks bent when thrust into water is really crooked is to request an explanation which presupposes a specific theory of optics. Only within such a theory can a statement of what is the case be given; and only within a certain theory will the bent

[7] See, for example, Vernon Van Dyke, "Values and Interests," *American Political Science Review*, 56, September, 1962, pp. 567–76.

stick be explained as an illusion. In the same fashion, whether light is regarded as particles or waves depends on one's theoretical framework. What light *really* is cannot be answered if it is meant as a request for the ontological status of light independent of theoretical perspectives; for only within one perspective or another do we know things.

In similar fashion, an ultimate justification for a value position cannot be given. When we judge that X is good for Y, we can relate it to Y in terms of means. This is a factual judgment of a contingent kind. But predicative judgments (X is good) can only be taken back to the act of commendation itself. To ask whether the favorable response is good cannot be answered if the request is meant to elicit a value judgment independent of responses. Only in terms of human response can we say what is good and what is not. Both facts and values, in this way, are always dependent on a conceptual system which can only be verified so far and no more.[8]

A formalization of the subjective model developed here will close out this part of the discussion. When I say that X is good, I mean that X has certain things about it, A, B, C, which bring about a favorable reaction from me. These things about X constitute my knowledgeable acquaintance with it, since any other features of X which I do not knowledgeably interact with cannot be meaningfully included as part of X, at least until I know about them. Knowing doesn't entail direct experience; but at least I must know the features in question to the extent that *if* I were directly acquainted with them, I would like X. This A, B, C of X can in any case be empirically identified and used as a quite sensible reason for X's goodness. That is, X is good because it has A, B, C (which evoke a favorable response from me valid within the limits of my knowledge).

[8] For an elaboration of the instrumental role of theories in both factual and value judgments, see Stephen Toulmin's *Reason in Ethics* (Cambridge: Cambridge University Press, 1960).

The subjective-response model is appropriate both in the predicative and attributive uses of good, which (we will recall) correspond to "X is good" and "X is a good Y." When we use good in an attributive sense we mean that whatever it takes to be a good Y, then X has it. This is a bit different from the kinds of arguments we have been pursuing up to now, which have referred largely to the predicative use of good. But the basic grounding of good in empirical features is even clearer with the "X is a good Y" model than that of "X is good." If we say that X has what it takes to be a good Y, then what it takes can surely be spelled out factually. The judgment is that X has certain features which justify inclusion within the category "good Y." This is a factual judgment which depends upon a prior predicative judgment that the features in question will be considered as good, which means (again) that these features have evoked a favorable response grounded in human knowledge.

THE CASE FOR VALUE-FREE SCIENCE: A REAPPRAISAL

No area has received more polemical attention than scientific neutrality. One of the main issues separating humanistic and positivist approaches in the social sciences is whether or not the social investigator can place his values in abeyance while involved in research. That this disagreement has also affected definitions of political inquiry need hardly be affirmed.[9] Yet the curious truth remains that no conceptual analysis can in itself definitively establish one thesis or another. As indicated in the earlier discussion of science and social analysis, only the possibility of methodological neutrality can be demonstrated, not the actuality.

This modest undertaking is what we will attempt here, for methodological neutrality is a feasible enterprise *if* it is

[9] Robert Dahl, *Modern Political Analysis* (Englewood Cliffs, N.J.: Prentice-Hall, 1963), pp. 93–110.

narrowly defined. This narrow definition must amount to nothing more than the claim that factual and value judgments can be distinguished, and therefore that it is possible for the research scientist to make factual judgments without making value judgments. No one can seriously argue that science is value-free. Even the phrase itself is absurd, for science (as we have seen) is itself realized only on the basis of a prior choice outside the system of science. But the question in empirical inquiry is whether it is possible to engage in factual investigation after the scientific enterprise has been assumed.

An examination of this question must be largely taxonomical. That is, arguments which deny the possibility of factual investigation must be classified according to whether they focus on the epistemological or normative dimensions of science. Such a classification system presupposes that factual and value judgments are different kinds of things in an empirical framework, a distinction which has just been demonstrated by a conceptual analysis of the term *good*. On this basis, a number of arguments commonly made to demonstrate the normative character of all science will be classified as discussions of factual judgments. In this way the possibility of methodological neutrality will be defended, but only as it is severely circumscribed.

In examining these arguments it is helpful to invoke one side of a theoretical dichotomy established very early in this discourse. This is the separation between substance and technique found in any formal inquiry. Many arguments can be classified according to whether they focus on *what* is studied, or *how* one conducts the study at issue. One important class of arguments against factual investigation admits neutrality in the analysis of nonhuman phenomena, but denies it to the social scientist. The rationale for these claims is the presence of intentionality in social phenomena, a property not possessed by physical phenomena. Only (the argument goes) as the analyst shares the purpose of social actors can he grasp what is happening in human behavior. Further, assuming these points of view entails adopting the values of the actors being studied, for the direction of choice and meaning in human activity constitutes the values in question.[10]

This argument has much to it in understanding the special problems of social investigation. Certainly it seriously qualifies the notion of a social science independent of its subject matter. Also it opens the door for the more intuitive moods of a *Verstehen* method. But however a phenomenon is approached—either with empathy or the more impersonal constructs of science—still the phenomenon must be recognized as an existent fact to be approached, and this recognition must be a factual and not a value judgment. Even the question of the adequacy of various approaches to the datum is a judgment of fact, in the sense that one is assessing to what degree a report embodies certain standards. This remains true whatever the source of the standards. So certain tasks must be performed with values suspended in any case.[11]

It is also not clear why an assumption of the actor's frame of reference leads inexorably to a value perspective. What is demonstrated in the response model of value is precisely the point that subjective viewing allows for a distinction between factual and value judgments. A value is a judgment including the ascription of favor or disfavor. Therefore it is *in part* an emotive response. Factual judgments need not ascribe favor. Since this distinction can be realized by a social participant, neither a subjective nor a more positivist approach to cultural data need necessarily involve value judgments, even though it may still be argued that a fuller understand-

[10] Lon Fuller argues this in "Human Purpose and Natural Law," *Natural Law Forum*, III (1958), pp. 68–76. Also see "A Rejoinder to Professor Nagel," *Natural Law Forum*, III (1958), pp. 83–104.

[11] Ernest Nagel, "Fact, Value, and Human Purpose," *Natural Law Forum*, IV (1959), pp. 26–43. Also, "On the Fusion of Fact and Value: A Reply to Professor Fuller," *Natural Law Forum*, III (1958), pp. 77–82.

ing of social reality ensues when emotive responses are directly embodied in the research scheme.

Another difficulty seeming to come out of the distinctiveness of cultural data is that of language. Empirical science requires descriptions of the phenomenon which is studied. Description must be couched in language. Hence empiricism carries with it a demand which is prior to the act of description itself: assigning linguistic symbols to the datum which is described, and recognizing genuine and spurious instances of this datum. So far this requirement holds for both the physical and social sciences. But the social analyst must deal with actors possessing verbal facility, and so his choice of words takes place within a framework of values formed outside his technical control. This can be taken to mean that any words used by the analyst possess normative overtones which cannot be suspended.

Two separate problems are presented in this argument. The first, that of assigning words to things in description, is true but trivial. Certainly language varies considerably in its normative overtones, but in basic linguistic expression a functional distinction holds between factual and value statements. To say that "X is yellow" may carry value implications in certain contexts, but we may reasonably expect this expression to be considerably more neutral than, say, "X is evil." This fundamental-distinction permits empirical science to be factual. Again, no term has constant flavor; nor is any word wholly neutral. But the question is whether description can proceed without some of the more pungent expressions. Surely it can, for a wide range of words is available which may be taken as value-free in many situations.

The second problem is more significant. Here the issue is a judgment of what datum is to count as an instance of the empirical concept directing analysis. Also, a judgment must be made of what, within the phenomenon categorized, is to be accepted as a true and what as a vulgarized manifestation.[12] A question thus arises of the proper standards to be used as a basis for these judgments, and also whether or not these judgments are normative in form. Two sources exist for the standards at issue. The first is that of the paradigm being validated. The second is the subjective point of view of the actors being studied. Neither source leads to a value judgment.

The first of these two sources is a technical one. Here the grounding for the required judgments may be explained in terms of perceived demands for data, conceptual inadequacies, or theoretical anomalies. But in any case the guiding principle is the research scheme and its requirements. The second source defines a construct and its veracity in terms of the perspective of actors in the social system. Here the task is one of accounting for (however imperfectly) the subjective meanings of social events. But, again, judgments in accordance with either of these two sets of standards are factual, not value, judgments. Value judgments are of the sort, "X is good or bad," not "X is more or less adequate as an analytic approach," or "X is or is not in accord with methodological standards."

We must not be confused with the notion of standards. Methodological neutrality has not been violated by the judgment that a technique or a conclusion is good when the meaning is correctness. What can be suspended in science is the predicative use of good, as, "X is good." What is consistent with this suspension is the attributive use of good, as, "X is a good Y." The attributive use of good may be regarded as a factual judgment that X has what it takes to be a good Y. It is normally a part of any factual inquiry. The predicative use of good is a value judgment. Hence, it is this latter use of good which is the issue in value-free inquiry. When scientists do not make this kind of judgment, they consider

[12] So Leo Strauss argues in *Natural Right and History, op. cit.*, pp. 49–62.

themselves involved in a factual investigation. This holds true even though predicative judgments may be factual objects of analysis, say as judgments made by members of a political system being studied. This suspension of the predicative use of good is all that can be meant by a value-free science.

To this line of argument a frequent objection is made. It takes the form of examples of the attributive use of good which appear quite certainly to be value judgments. These are of the type, "This is a good political system." But, however strong this kind of an example may appear to be, any instance of the attributive use of good may remain a factual judgment. In the example cited, the judgment may be taken as an assertion that this political system possesses certain features which allow it to be subsumed under the general class of good political systems. Hence the judgment may be a factual determination that these features are present in the specific political system being so judged. Of course a prior value judgment of a predicative type is implied in this factual judgment, for only as the features in question have been judged to be good can the general class of good political systems be established. This means that the factual judgment is of the sort: *if* these features are what constitute good political systems, then this political system possesses them and is entitled to be called good. Whether the features are really good or not, which can be translated into whether the predicative evaluation is true, is a separate judgment. Whether political investigators can make such judgments in the form of recommendations will be discussed later.

PURPOSE AND POLITICS

One form of the argument laying out a value base for all political investigation is grounded in the ascription of purpose to human society. It is put forward by Leo Strauss, and it goes something like this. Political events can be distinguished from other phenomena only by designating such events as relevant to the polis. This presupposes an explicit definition of society. But society cannot be defined without reference to its purpose. Hence all political analysis must take as a fundamental concept the end or goal of society.[13] This argument is directed primarily against the nonethical character of modern political analysis, but in postulating an ethical content to all political inquiry it binds political science to a common framework; for the argument amounts to the assertion that unless one investigates purposes one is not doing political analysis.

The heart of this argument is lodged in the concept of purpose. What it means will determine how we are to take what Strauss is saying. Two definitions are possible. First, the concept can be empirical. Second, it can be normative. In the first case we are talking about the factual goals of a political system, which, in turn, may be either explicit or implicit. In the second case, purpose means the goal which society *ought* to have whether it in fact has it or not.

Both of these definitions are troublesome for Strauss's argument. We have no reason, first, to believe that an explicit factual purpose is a necessary part of a society's existence. At the risk of introducing an uncomfortable factor into teleological considerations, we may conclude from empirical surveys that political systems can function without any explicit purpose, at least in the sense that most members of the system need not have system goals of which they are aware.[14] The question of purpose as an *ought* imposed on society independent of factual states is even more difficult to understand. Unless the *ought* is related in some way to the polity we cannot take it as the purpose of the polity.

[13] Leo Strauss, *What is Political Philosophy?* (Glencoe, Ill.: The Free Press, 1959).

[14] Angus Campbell *et al.*, *The American Voter* (New York: John Wiley & Sons, 1960), p. 543.

What Strauss seems to mean by purpose is an existent state not necessarily recognized by the members of a polity. The end of the state is a fundamental ordering of the body politic which is implicit in any actual situation. This is the *regime*, or the form which gives society its character. Every polity in this view possesses a regime, since every society is organized along some style of life. Such an argument rests on the assumption that life is activity directed towards some goal; and, accordingly, social life is activity directed toward the goal which is pursued by society. But in order to pursue a specific goal, the argument continues, society must be ordered in accordance with that goal. Hence, from goal-oriented activity the existence of an order in society is deduced.

Two points must be made. First, society is not taken as monolithic in this argument. A variety of regimes is assumed, each of which raises a claim which is more universal than the boundaries of any given society. Second, the regime functions as a connection between the *ought* of purpose and the factual state; for the goal of society is taken as a norm which is then reflected in the existent order of society. These two points lead (for Strauss) to the essential nature of political inquiry, which is to arbitrate between conflicting regimes. This is done in the initial act of identifying a datum as political, for by doing this the political analyst has related the datum to a regime; and, also, the analyst has engaged in normative activity as well, inasmuch as the regime is the normative goal of society.

It must be pointed out here that this argument is a much stronger claim than the assertion that political science *can* arbitrate between conflicting regimes; or, that is, that it can successfully function as a normative inquiry. The claim here is that it can do nothing else; and this essential feature of political analysis binds all political science, whatever the historical period. The main difference in this thesis between old and new political inquiry is this: that classical theorists recognized the necessary value content of their inquiry while modern theorists do not. But whether recognized or not, any political analysis is bound to relate data to one or another regime as a necessary condition for doing political inquiry.

Three questions will serve to assess the merits of this argument. First, is the order characteristic of any society possible without the introduction of purpose? Second, is it necessary to relate a datum to the whole of society in order to study social phenomena? Third, can the political scientist engage in a kind of inquiry which is distinct from the partisan claims of those supporting one regime or another? These are not by any means arbitrary questions asked in an impartial manner. They are designed to elicit anticipated answers, but in doing so they will elaborate and qualify the argument we are discussing.

The initial question is whether order and purpose can only be taken as complementary sides of the same concept. The answer is no. By the order of a society we usually mean a formal disposition or array of its parts. Purpose suggests an intended or desired result. It might well be true that a purposeful collectivity must be ordered in accordance with that purpose, although there are good reasons for not thinking this (such as the fact that purpose can be abstract and totally unrealized). But this is of no concern here. It is clear that the order defining a factual society can be taken separate from purpose.

The strength of the dissent from taking society only in terms of purpose is that purpose need not be denied. It may even be accepted as a necessary feature of human life, paralleling at the level of the collectivity the intentional character of human consciousness we discussed earlier. But taking purpose as sufficient in itself to define society is too much. Other considerations, such as spatial location and contemporaneity, can constitute a definition. It is in this category of considerations separate from purpose that the notion of order must be placed. Purpose is not shelved. But it is also not necessary to consider goals or ends in order to consider the formal array of society.

The second question, that of the necessity involved in relating a datum to the whole of society, is of this same general sort. Must we, that is, always subsume social data under the rubric of the societal whole in order for the data to qualify as social? To break this posed necessity is easy enough, for only one method of designating social phenomena other than that of the entire social system need be adduced. For this purpose only, let us say that an act can be viewed as social if it involves more than one person. The attendant difficulties with this proposal can be left aside, for all that it is intended to demonstrate is that concepts can be postulated for handling social phenomena other than that of the entire social system.

We need not even deny that such a concept may finally lead, from logical necessity, to the whole of society. Nor does this argument deny the efficacy of the whole social order as a conceptual reference. But it does mean that a social datum can be seen at any particular time as considerably less than a direct adjunct of the social whole; and also that there are levels of analysis in social inquiry which can be conducted in reference to fragments within society taken on their own, apart from the entire social order. Again, it is the question of necessity which must be qualified. To say that *all* social analysis must be pitched at the level of the aggregate is to ignore the special and middle-range generalities which treat human interactions.

The final question can be pursued in the same way. Given that the social system is characterized by conflicting regimes, it does not follow from this that social inquiry must be partisan. It may even be the case that the conceptual framework adopted by the analyst coincides with any one of a number of regimes. But coincidence of this sort is not advocacy. A concept adopted for explanatory purposes may be taken precisely as that, and not as an end which ought to be realized. To deny the possibility of nonpartisan inquiry of this sort is to succumb (cf. Mannheim) to one's own argument, for only as inquiry begins to escape partisanship can we speak with any degree of assurance of what we are saying. Further, any claim which merges inquiry with partisanship on a necessary level denies the distinction between factual and value judgments established earlier in this discussion.

Let us be clear that the answers to these three questions are not proofs of a traditional kind. We have not, that is, built up a compelling case against the version of inquiry promulgated by Leo Strauss. But the alternatives drawn up demonstrate that Strauss' decrees need not be taken as both necessary and sufficient features of political inquiry. To claim, as Strauss does, that all political inquiry must be such a way and no other is to assume the burden of proof for the case. It cannot be done by simple fiat. Hence, the response to any severe circumscription of inquiry is to demonstrate that a great deal of activity normally considered as political analysis will be excluded, and to request reasons of a compelling sort for such a severe definition. So far we have not encountered these reasons in any compelling form.

One thing, however, must be made perfectly clear at this stage: the primary focus of political inquiry on value-directed agencies is not being denied by these arguments against Strauss. The issue is the effect of this focus on the investigating process. It seems perfectly reasonable (in contradistinction to Strauss' assertions) to study factually actors who are engaged in prescribing or advocating values. Hence values enter political inquiry as factual objects to be investigated (actor X has value Y), but this is no reason to conclude that political analysis itself is *necessarily* tied to one set of observable values or another. The very distinction established earlier between descriptive and value terms denies this necessity.

THE CULTURAL NORM

How far can we get with methodological neutrality? Not very far at all. This discourse has demonstrated that factual inquiry is possible. But the narrowness of the definition must be emphasized. It amounts, in effect, to the claim that factual judgments may be made without value judgments being made; or that the social scientist is not compelled to engage in "practical evaluations of the unsatisfactory or satisfactory character of phenomena subject to our influence."[15] When the analyst moves from specific judgments to theoretical explanations, the matter becomes considerably more complicated. But there remains in any case a factual foundation *within* the point of view assumed, and we should be aware that it exists. To deny that it does exist amounts to the absurdity that factual and value judgments cannot be distinguished at all.

It is the cultural perspective which gives all inquiry its value content. Theoretical categories are constructs of the analyst imposed on phenomena to give the phenomena meaning. We know by now that they are not constructed in a vacuum, but are dependent on human relationships to yield them. All inquiry is not a smooth continuum from society to reflection. Social investigation can turn ordinary categories of meaning inside out. But the necessary condition for a social science is society. Hence, all factual inquiry is grounded in a cultural framework; and the separation between facts and values can be realized only within theoretical views containing the general predilections of a culture. We are, in answer to an earlier question, biased in the long run, even though it is possible to be unbiased in the short run.

Escaping the long-run bias is as difficult as getting out of one's skin. For this reason any formulae advanced for

[15] Max Weber, *The Methodology of the Social Sciences*, trans. by Edward Shils and Henry Finch (Glencoe, Ill.: The Free Press, 1949) p. 1.

totally neutral research must demonstrate how we can account for our cultural values, not shed them. Accounting entails awareness, and so the task of seeing things with as little bias as possible involves knowing ourselves as much as possible, and stating this knowledge so that others may allow for our values when taking stock of what we have done. The idea conveyed by this process is clear enough: if we can't get rid of our bias, we can at least compensate for it by making it explicit.

But, like Polonius' admonitions to Laertes, any directions for complete neutrality become increasingly peculiar as one scrutinizes them. For one thing, it is obviously impossible to reveal totally the values embodied in any point of view. The revelation itself (as we have seen) embodies one point of view or another, and so we are back once more to the paradox of Mannheim's sociology of knowledge. Even given, however, that partial revelation is better than none at all, a crucial question remains: how is one to reveal one's fundamental values? Or, put another way, is there some test by which we can say with assurance that a person has authentically revealed the deepest of his commitments?

David Easton in *The Political System* outlines two operational procedures for getting at this question. First, he argues that if a person constructs an ideal political order, then this ideal polity will reveal many of the fundamental values of its creator. Plato, we may suppose, is writ large in his *Republic*. Second, Easton asserts that if an individual is placed in a situation where he is forced to make ultimate choices on ultimate grounds, then he will—by definition, really—make clear his deepest values by what he does. Only in such extreme instances, the model of a perfect state and what might be called an existential situation, can we be reasonably sure that ultimate or categorical norms have been revealed.[16]

But the difficulties with these tests, or any tests at all, are quickly evident. (Many of them are recognized by Easton

[16] Easton, *op. cit.* pp. 229–32.

himself.) The primary view of values as a hierarchy built up from the base of an ultimate commitment can itself be called in question. It is true that one's explicit values may be pushed back until one is forced to admit to an emotive affirmation. If I am asked why I value, say, the family as a social unit, and I answer that it makes for psychological stability, then I still may be asked why I value psychological stability. After enough of these questions one may get to some caterogical norm of one sort or another. But why need this be taken as *the* ultimate commitment from which all other norms are issued?

Certainly no logical, or necessary, relationship exists between a categorical norm and intermediate values. From the statement by an individual to the effect that he loves human life, one cannot deduce the specific conditions that this individual will embrace as a way of realizing this norm. It has even been demonstrated that values held in the abstract by an individual may be in a state of contradiction with the same individual's concrete behavior, and yet he may be none the worse for wear.[17] Nor do we have any reason to suppose that one ultimate commitment exists as a foundation for all other values. An individual may have several basic commitments, many of them categorical. He may, in fact, have no basic commitments at all for his value judgments.

All of this may seem to be of only marginal relevance for the theorist of value who is interested in revealing the logical structure of value judgments. But the observation remains: if value judgments may be made without a hierarchy of mutually consistent values, then we cannot factually root out the foundations of bias in any definitive fashion. No foundation, however defined, may even exist. Or, if it

[17] Gunnar Myrdal, *An American Dilemma* (New York: Harper & Bros., 1944). See also the wealth of literature on cognitive dissonance. Among the many excellent books in this area is Leon Festinger's *A Theory of Cognitive Dissonance* (Evanston, Ill.: Row Peterson, 1957).

does, it may not be coherently related to explicit judgments. The standards of logical consistency may yield certain conceptual truths about value reasoning, but securing a state of methodological neutrality is a factual undertaking which must, therefore, take into account the factual possibilities of self-revelation.

Even if we find an individual with a logically consistent hierarchy of values, any factual indicators for such values can, at best, only partially reveal the values in question. Sometimes no general judgments can be made at all. Let us suppose that a man is brave in battle, and cowardly in front of the House Committee on Un-American Activities. Is the man courageous, or not? It is impossible to say. Yet each of these situations may demand extreme choices. The problem is this: no one situation can ever be said to realize in definitive fashion the values possessed by an individual, for any value yields an open class of factual indicators. The same observation holds true for the construction of an ideal political system. Even Plato, we must remember, had his *Laws*.

The conclusion to be drawn from this, however, is not totally negative. Any reflection is better than none at all; and even open indicators are helpful. We know considerably more about a man when we have seen him perform in two extreme situations comparable to war and the HUAC hearings, even though definitive judgments are not possible. It is in the notion of ultimate commitments that trouble lies, not in the attempt to reveal cultural direction. Like all empirical enterprises, this one must remain uncertain and modest, and also somewhere within the tentative framework which makes empirical inquiry possible.

POLICY-MAKING:
THE VALIDITY OF RECOMMENDATIONS

A question of considerable importance in political inquiry is the status and general relevance of statements which recommend one course of action or another. This question is distinct from the discussion on methodological neutrality, for in whatever way one studies the polity it is still possible to ask whether one should make value judgments about the way the political system ought to be, and whether these judgments have some general validity. These two discussions would overlap only if one argued that *any* study of politics is prescriptive, or that factual statements are always recommendations. But this thesis has been demonstrated in the preceding discussion as untenable.

Thus the question is this: however accurate our information is about the political system, can we construct *oughts* of policy-making which are more than statements of personal preference? The urgency of this question arises from the nature of political events. The political analyst studies actors who prescribe values. Even, therefore, in the most neutral of political inquiries, values enter as objects of investigation. This does not, as we have seen, mean that political analysts must make prescriptive judgments themselves. One can factually study (within the limits established earlier) a value-directed process. But it poses a certain peculiarity. The modern student of politics scrutinizes a system which makes value judgments of the most general and compelling sort, yet the intellectual framework directing this scrutiny includes the assumption that values are nothing more than the personal preferences of the judging subject.

Even the positivist in political inquiry, however, is not totally paralyzed in the area of value. Clarification and means-ends judgments are legitimate goals within a purely emotivist framework. Weber, as we might expect, has delineated the role of the scientist in value theory. First, the scientist may unravel the axioms from which normative propositions are derived. Second, he may demonstrate the theoretical relationships holding between various value theses. Third, he may indicate the factual consequences which the realization of an evaluation might have, either in consequence of being bound to certain indispensable means, or as a result of the repercussions following from the actualization of the norm itself.[18]

Observations of factual consequences have an especially direct bearing on the status of an evaluation if the evaluation is directed toward changing some state of affairs. Empirical analysis can demonstrate the impossibility of securing the desired change, or predict the probability of success. Also, it can reveal whatever conditions ought to be taken into account in attempting to obtain the desired end. Even after the process of obtaining what one wants has begun, an empirical investigation may reveal new value-axioms, as well as new sets of means and relevant conditions. At every stage of evaluation a scientific survey is at least relevant, and often necessary.

But, of course, all of this is factual inquiry. Further, such inquiry is relevant only as an end is presupposed. About the value of the end, or goal, empirical inquiry cast in the positivist mold cannot say. It is outside the purview of science.[19] For such an assessment, Weber suggests, one can turn to faith, which provides the only means to judge the validity of goals in themselves.[20] "It can never be the task of an empirical science to provide binding norms and ideals from which directives for immediate practical activity can be derived."[21]

This argument is, however, extremely odd. The norm of efficiency can be realized only as the end which is pursued has been determined. This means that the establishment of a goal is a prior necessity to the conduct of means-end inquiry, for only as we know where we are going can we say what is the best way to get there. For the self-contained empiricist this leads to a dilemma. A positivist science cannot

[18] Weber, *The Methodology of the Social Sciences, op. cit.*, p. 20.
[19] Brecht, *Political Theory, op. cit.*
[20] Weber, *The Methodology of the Social Sciences, op. cit.* p. 55.
[21] *Ibid.*, p. 52.

get going until something has been settled which the positivist claims cannot be intellectually settled in the first place: goals for activity.

There is a way out of this muddle. It amounts to a stretching of the notion of verification in science to reasonable proportions. The claim that scientific inquiry can do nothing to recommend one goal or another is based on the assumption that only two sharp and exclusive modes of verification exist: analytic and empirical. This is, as we have seen (Chapter II), a mistake. The analytic–empirical distinction is neither sharp nor exclusive. Many propositions can only be classified in the context in which they are uttered, and more informal means of verification are common features of human intercourse. People do make choices; and these choices are often justified by individuals to each other, even though such justification may not satisfy the hard requirements of a positivist verification.

Science itself is conducted on the general basis of justification. No matter how strictly we define scientific verifications, we still mean that reasons are adduced for saying that something is so. Sentences are not verified like pieces in a jigsaw puzzle, to be judged true if they fit neatly in place and false if they do not. When a proposition has been established scientifically, this means that evidence has been accepted which convinces us that the proposition is true. Only rarely does the evidence yield a clear case. In the same fashion one goal or another may be chosen on the basis of reasons which can be adduced for saying that it is better than another goal. The strict verification or nonverification of the goal is an inappropriate issue. In *all* forms of verification we are supplying reasons, as we do when we justify value choices.

One important way to justify values is to refer to facts, or what we commonly agree to be the case about something. A sharply imposed fact–value distinction would disallow such a move. But we must remember that the distinction between facts and values is logical only, meaning that knowledge is never a sufficient condition for a value judgment. Logic, however, is not everything. What we know certainly has a bearing on the kind of value judgment we make, and whether it is a worthwhile judgment or not. Otherwise we are stuck with the silly thesis that knowing nothing about X is the same as knowing everything when it comes to judging the goodness of X.

How silly a complete separation between facts and values truly is was demonstrated in the bomb example, where an individual may be unknowingly judging as "good" the source of his own destruction. Only as we possess factual knowledge can we sensibly make value judgments; and we justify these judgments in part on the basis of our factual knowledge. Further, this loose but necessary relationship between facts and values yields the intellectual framework which makes values capable of justification; for any definition of knowledge must include standards for determining correctness and error. Hence, values can be examined, selected, and defended on the basis of a factual investigation.

The man, for example, who knows about atmospheric results in bomb testing is in a better position to assess the value of such testing than one who does not, even though someone else may later discover another factor to be taken into account, and so on. But in each case a level of knowledge may be predicated as a basis for value judgments. Again, no sufficient relationship exists between facts and values. We are all too aware of what we consider hideous acts grounded in correct knowledge. But a necessary relationship exists in the sense that empirical knowledge constitutes a base for determining when affective responses are accurate. Otherwise we must accept the synonymity of *likes* and *values*, which (as we saw in the bomb example) it is not possible to do. Only with cognitive experience can we begin to say which *likes* are correct, and which are not.

The sad truth of empiricism is that absolutely certain

judgments are not possible. But nihilism does not follow from this. Many factual judgments are of such high probability that they may be regarded as completely certain. (It is precisely this stability that allows the world to function at all.) Further, the tenuous state of empirical judgments is not a feature simply of value judgments, but of both facts and values. If we do not know the real good in an empiricist framework, neither do we know the real object. Or, put more strongly, the good is corrigible in the same way that the fact is corrigible, which is that both must be seen as probable and never certain. But we need not infer from this that all things are possible, even though a great many might be; for the same likelihood that we know things also furnishes the rationale for defining the good in specific human situations.

On this account of the relationship between facts and values it is possible to make recommendations which can be judged correct or incorrect. The general claim that the political investigator cannot do this is based on an erroneous notion of the fact-value dualism. Factual and value judgments do have a bearing upon one another, even if the connection is not a deductive one. It must be remembered that the tight bindings of logic constitute a rare form of relationship, and certainly are not characteristic of science generally. The scientist who waits for deductive proofs will, in all likelihood, wait a long time indeed. In political inquiry—a subject which focuses on the prescriptive dimension of society—it is especially odd to find values excluded because they do not yield to axiomatic formulations.

POLITICS AND VALUES

The role of values in political investigation has been shown to be multiple. First, values enter the cultural framework within which all political analysis takes place. This is the long-range bias of any intellectual undertaking. Further, the cultural framework is a necessary condition for social analysis and therefore cannot be placed in abeyance. Second, values (as judgments made by actors) are factual objects of inquiry. This particular function of values is of more import in political than in social analysis, inasmuch as the political investigator focuses on that apparatus which is prescriptive for society generally. Third, values are a part of political inquiry in the recommendations that the political analyst can make in policy-making areas.

It has also been demonstrated that factual and value judgments are distinguished from each other on the basis of the responses (affective v. cognitive) of the perceiving subject. Further, political inquiry can be value-free *within* a cultural framework to the extent that these two kinds of judgments are different. But, even though they are different kinds of judgments, facts and values are related in the sense that the cognitive part of experience makes possible the separation of *likes* and *values*. Recommendations thus become possible on the basis of expertise, even though expertise is not a sufficient condition for normative judgments.

CHAPTER VI

Political Inquiry

PROBLEMS AND ALTERNATIVES

Any definition of political inquiry must assume one of two forms: empirical or normative. The first form is a descriptive summary of what goes on factually under the broad title "political inquiry." In the second case one is stipulating what political inquiry ought to be, whether in fact it is this or not. A little of both of these kinds of definitions will be attempted here. The common threads which connect classical with modern theory will be traced in summary fashion. But, also, some admonitions and recommendations will emerge. Such an enterprise is perfectly legitimate in view of the last chapter.

Attempts to define political inquiry must come to terms with the realism that all forms of investigation perform not one, but many functions. For this reason it is pointless to say that one set of activities constitutes the study of politics,

187

and nothing else will do. At least two functions of political inquiry have been identified so far: explanation and recommendation. But, on the other hand, it is possible to isolate common features of all political investigation, although no one common feature can be taken as the full definition of political analysis. Whatever is constant is a characteristic which allows us to say that we are engaged in political investigation, even though we may be doing a lot of things at once. *This* kind of definition is possible.

It is necessary to make this obvious point in view of the wealth of literature which has neglected it. Definitions of political inquiry have centered on power, groups, decision making, systems, communications, and other more parochial concepts.[1] Many are structured severely. The conundrums generated by attempts to say *precisely* what political inquiry is will not be dealt with here. It is doubtful that such a definition can be formed, given the fact of multiple functions in inquiry. What will be attempted here is the identification of general characteristics in the absence of which one cannot study politics. We will, that is, postulate necessary but not sufficient features.

Only on the mistaken assumption that theories fit the world in an objective state of truth or falsity is it possible to envisage a strict definition in any form of inquiry. The systematic scrutiny of experience is, in contrast to the objective view, always a utility construct of the perceiving subject. This is the instrumental role of theories so familiar to us by now. Hence, given that technique and substance are generated by human beings as a way of making their experiences intelligible, we have no reason to think that narrowly con-

---

[1] As an example of the wide range of approaches to the study of politics, see Roland Young's *Approaches to the Study of Politics* (Evanston, Ill.: Northwestern University Press, 1962). For a quick look at some of the problems generated by attempts to define political inquiry precisely, see James C. Charlesworth, ed., *A Design for Political Science* (Philadelphia: The American Academy of Political and Social Science, 1966).

trived definitions will have any neat criteria by which to say that political reality has been—finally—enclosed. Both political theory and political behavior, as empirical occurrences, must remain open-ended.

This does not mean that inquiry is without standards. Investigation cannot proceed without a set of criteria for assessing evidence and arriving at conclusions. But the judgment of the analyst in constructing and applying these criteria cannot be overemphasized. An example from the physical sciences is often used to demonstrate this point. If a zoologist is proceeding in accordance with the empirical law that a certain animal is one color and he encounters a creature that fulfills all of the requirements for that animal except that the creature is another color, then he is faced with two alternatives: either he must judge that the creature is not the animal in question, or he must change the theoretical structure with which he explains the world.

Political actors, to be sure, are not animals that a zoologist would normally study. But this same interaction between the theorist and his experiences (or between theory and data) is common to all empirical inquiry. Each is changed by the other.[2] What is political is defined as political by the political investigator (with the qualification that social analysts, unlike zoologists, must take into account how actors define politics). In turn, the conceptual framework is conditioned and refined by phenomena as it accounts for events. Closed definitions of political inquiry are therefore impossible, for the study of politics is an open and continuing process. The standards which are found in any factual investigation must be conditioned by the investigation.

One unfortunate way to avoid this fundamental dialectic between theory and data is to rely on concepts which are ambiguous. When words can mean anything, experience cannot change them. Much of what passes for political

[2] Robert Merton, *Social Theory and Social Structure* (Glencoe, Ill.: The Free Press, 1957), pp. 85–117.

terminology carries such a liability.[3] Part of this difficulty can be explained away as the result of nonsystematic thinking. But a central ambiguity is also built into any attempt at a narrow definition of political inquiry, and this is the hard fact that political concepts refer to a very large number of different events.

Power and authority, for example, can be used to refer to phenomena ranging from the family to the state.[4] Even if some separation is established between political and nonpolitical units (where, for example, the family is excluded from consideration), the variance among kinds of political actors is often quite high. This is not so severe a problem in homogeneous societies where political behavior might be identified with the activities of a few actors. But in pluralistic societies the problem is acute. It is further compounded in system definitions of political phenomena, where nongovernmental agents are included in the definition of politics.[5]

Further, the fact that events affect one another in numerous ways makes it difficult to distinguish political from nonpolitical units. If a father criticizes the Supreme Court in the privacy of his home, is this a political event? Suppose it affects the future voting pattern of his son? These questions are obvious ones, and yet they readily demonstrate the impossibility of *strictly* separating the political system from the general social system. A definition of political inquiry, if it is to rely on substantive focus and not technical considerations, must conceptualize politics as a continuum from the social to the political, and not as a dichotomy. Like the zoologist encountering his strange animal, the political in-

[3] This fact was recognized by George Orwell in his stimulating essay, "Politics and the English Language," reprinted in *The Orwell Reader* (New York: Harcourt, Brace and World) pp. 355–66.

[4] Sheldon Wolin, *Politics and Vision* (Boston: Little, Brown & Co., 1960), p. 4. Wolin trenchantly discusses this and similar definitional problems in his opening chapter.

[5] See the discussion in Chapter III.

vestigator must count on engaging gray zones where his categories never quite fit.

THEORETICAL COMPARISONS

A general outline of social inquiry has been sketched in the course of this work. It will function as the backdrop to the identification of what is necessary to the conduct of political investigation. The picture of the investigatory process which has been delineated is that of an activity with rules and boundaries. On the basis of these rules, certain moves are permitted and others are denied. But assuming the set of rules in the first place is a move which is outside the game of inquiry, and therefore neither permitted nor denied. Only on the basis of an already accepted framework of rules can the legitimacy of intellectual procedures be determined.

This delineation casts inquiry into two complementary, but distinct, categories: tacit and overt. In the explicit dimension may be found research methods and epistemological assumptions. These assumptions may be pressed reflectively (the regressing sequence of *why* questions) until one moves outside the framework of rules by which methods and assumptions can be defined. It is this limiting characteristic of all inquiry, i.e., the presence of boundaries, that yields the tacit ingredient; for as boundaries exist, so too must an area exist beyond these boundaries. The tacit foundation of inquiry is thus the intuitive, or noncognitive, foundation by which rule-directed activity is accepted in the first place.

Also, a distinction holds between subject and object in any form of inquiry; or, as phrased in this discussion, between method and substance. A word of qualification is needed for this distinction. When we say that method and substance are separate, this observation refers to inquiry only. In much of what might be called direct experience technique *is* substance, for *doing* amounts to the experience itself. What else is sex but method? Some experiences are so direct that no intellectual framework is required at all, as Wittgenstein illustrated with the example of physical pain. But all inquiry is reflective, not direct, and hence entails a separation between method and substance. When I live, I *am* the experience. But when I reflect, I detach myself from the lived experience in order to scrutinize it. Investigation is therefore distinct from what is investigated.[6]

The changes which have taken place in political analysis historically have occurred, as we might expect, at the explicit level. Classical political theory possesses an epistemology which is different from that set of rules defining modern inquiry. Further, the experiences which are conceptualized within each framework differ in quality to some degree. As the rules for seeing the world change, so does much of the world which is seen. Most especially, the role of values *as recommendations* in social methodology has changed. Political inquiry from classical through medieval thought is largely ethical in purpose. From some of Machiavelli's work, but more importantly from Hume forward, political theory has been only marginally concerned with ethical theory.[7]

---

[6] The absorption of ordinary experience is expressed by Jean-Paul Sartre in the following passage: "When I run after a streetcar, when I look at the time, when I am absorbed in contemplating a portrait, there is no I. There is consciousness *of the streetcar—having-to-be-overtaken,* etc., and non-positional consciousness of consciousness. In fact, I am then plunged into the world of objects; it is they which constitute the unity of my consciousness; it is they which present themselves with values, with attractive and repellent qualities—but *me,* I have disappeared; I have annihilated myself." Quoted from J.-P. Sartre, *The Transcendence of the Ego,* trans. by F. Williams and R. Kirkpatrick, (New York: Noonday Press, 1957) partially cited by M. Natanson in *Literature, Philosophy and the Social Sciences* (The Hague: Martinus Nyhoff, 1962), p. 20. It is my claim—not necessarily held by Sartre—that any form of inquiry is a severing of this ego-object identification.

[7] This is an observation on which almost every theorist would agree, from Strauss to the empirical political analysts. The dividing question is, what are we to make of it?

All of these observations have been discussed in the course of this work. What has not been elaborated is the range of constant features found in all political inquiry. To say that the explicit methodology of inquiry has changed is not equivalent to the statement that inquiry itself has totally changed. The two other dimensions of political investigation generate the similarities which hold political analysis together. First, all political investigation (no matter what the conceptual framework) focuses on the value-directive apparatus of society. Second, both classical and modern political investigation rely on an intuitive, or emotive, base to give direction to the explicit rules constituting the differences between them.

THE FOCUS OF INQUIRY

Participants make choices. They do not do so in all circumstances, nor always with good sense (however defined). But the study of society is the study of creatures who select some things instead of others. Not even in a totally deterministic model of human behavior can this be denied; for even causally determined choices remain instances of selective behavior. To say that one is forced to choose is not tantamount to saying that one has not chosen. This observation amounts to a point made earlier: values enter the study of society as objects to be investigated. Hence, the substantive focus of all social theory includes, as facts, the norms which are left out of a positivist methodology.

What distinguishes social events from political events is the element of compulsion. This feature can be delineated on a scale moving from personal to external values. A personal value judgment is a simple preference, or emotive response. This is the ascription of good which was discussed earlier. Values begin to be external when they include prescription, or *oughts*. This compulsive feature may be a psychological variable, as when I feel I ought to do something because I think that it is right. But an *ought* always originates external to the primary system of desire; for an *ought* can only be realized when one has a disposition to do something other than that which the normative element directs.[8] The most external form of value is the association of the normative with another, or where the directive to do something originates with someone other than the self. This is the point at which politics begins: where the *ought* becomes an external *must*.

Several qualifying remarks will put this observation into the correct perspective. First, it is not, nor is it intended to be, new. We are engaged at this point in an empirical identification. I propose that the depiction of politics as external prescription is a constant theme in political inquiry ranging from the classical to the modern. Further, the identification of this theme does not complete the definition of political inquiry. Much more (as we shall see) is needed. But every other feature of the focus of political inquiry is a variable of the theorist under consideration. What is constant is a process only: political behavior is, fundamentally, that form of behavior where norms are enforced on any person from a source outside that person.

Also, it is obvious that all social behavior is not included in this process. Two extreme sets of circumstances where the enforcement of norms does not occur remain outside the purview of politics. One is a social situation of perfect harmony in which the harmony is a derivative of autonomous individuals. Each, that is, does exactly what he wants to do, and the result is a natural ordering of activities. Adam Smith's "invisible hand" is analogous. The other is a state of autonomous behavior which results in disharmony. Neither case fits the definition of politics identified here, for

---

[8] This separation between *ought* and *desire* goes back at least to the *Republic*. Plato sees reason as that which intervenes between desire and its satisfaction.

no enforcement occurs. In the first instance a utopian natural state of cooperation is described. In the second situation, anarchy or socially accepted violence is depicted. A political system does not exist in either situation.

Distinctions which must be made between more ordinary social events and the political order entail additional layers to the prescriptive basis of politics. These distinctions must be made for the simple reason that the prescriptive process goes on in areas and in ways which it would be absurd to regard as part of the political system. A thief robs a store. A father sends his child to bed. A teacher expels a student from class. In each of these examples norms are externally enforced. But in none of these cases would we want to say that political action is taking place.

The basis on which we designate these cases as nonpolitical must be something more than prescription alone. Four other distinctions are normally imposed on the basic behavioral act in politics: public–private; comprehensive–partial; categorical–contingent; legitimate–illegitimate. All of these additional considerations are continuums found in the assignment of political meaning to prescriptive behavior. What the concepts mean and where one is to locate politics on the array of positions between each of these concepts is, again, answered differently by different theorists. Further, not all of the four distinctions are always found in the conceptualization of politics. Primitive political systems do not often yield a separation of private and public. Relations between political systems may not involve categorical prescription. But the imposition of some, and often all, of these additional categories is what makes prescriptive behavior a political event.

None of the four distinctions added to prescriptive behavior can be established sharply. What is presented to us in the task of defining politics is a set of necessary requirements which, nevertheless, cannot be definitively satisfied.

The question of public or private events illustrates this point. Since Aristotle, Western theorists have recognized that a household is different than the polity. But getting at the point where events are part of one and not the other poses a peculiar difficulty. It has already been alluded to in the earlier example of a father's exhortations affecting the voting behavior of his son. It can be generally stated in this way: establishing the precise point where public and private events are distinct entails splintering the obvious connection holding between institutions which are comprised of the same people. The private individual is, after all, also the public citizen.

With the thought in mind that the four distinctions *are* continuums, not dichotomies, the remaining three can be defined. By comprehensive–partial is meant societal effectiveness. Control is exercised over the society embraced by the political system. Easton, for example, speaks of authoritative allocation for *all* of society. As we might expect, politics is not always totally comprehensive. Intermediate groups, such as local governments, are also part of the political process. But intermediate activity is still a controlling system for intermediate territory, even though not necessarily complete; and, further, at some stage one is able to refer to the comprehensive political unit. Otherwise some form of civil conflict or anarchic state exists.

The third distinction, categorical–contingent, is another dimension of the control concept. But instead of comprehensiveness, this concept indicates that the political system is the final arbiter for conflicting desires. It may help to think of comprehensiveness as a horizontal dimension of control, and categorical as a vertical dimension. The political system, as a categorical representation, is the last step up the vertical dimension. This does not mean that dissent is impossible, for one can always object even to decisions which are implemented in final form. But the political system is ultimate in the sense that no other practicable recourse is available for appeal. This is, in one form or another, the concept of sovereignty.

The final distinction, legitimate–illegitimate, is a tired subject already treated in the discussion of system states.[9] What is gotten at with this notion is the basis upon which we can judge that a political system is not a gang of thugs who have seized control. It is quite permissible, of course, to answer that if a gang of thugs seizes effective control it *is* the political system. In this case we have simply identified legitimacy with control, and established the distinction by merging it with another. Whether this is the best way to go about answering the question of legitimacy is of no concern here. The point is that in some fashion one must say when and on what basis the exercise of power becomes the exercise of authority.

The various ways in which theorists have attempted to determine the four distinctions added to prescriptive behavior will not be traced here. The task would be a separate work in itself. Our concern is, fortunately, more circumscribed. It is, put briefly, to identify the constant features which constitute the focus of all political inquiry. We have, with this thought in mind, defined the object of political investigation as a prescriptive process with some, or all of, four features not possessed by other kinds of prescriptive behavior. See the illustration on page 198.

As prescriptive behavior is public, comprehensive, categorical, and/or legitimate, it is political. Further, *all* political theorists focus on prescriptive behavior. It is, in this way, a constant. Once such behavior has been established, the four concepts delineated above are imposed on the phenomena. How these concepts are defined and applied helps to distinguish one political theorist from another. But, whatever the variations, political inquiry is always the study of value-directed behavior. Hence, to define what it is we are doing

---

[9] See Chapter III.

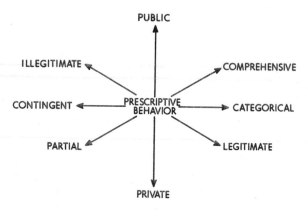

when we engage in political investigation, it is necessary to analyze the meaning of value; for it is, on this account, the fundamental feature of all political inquiry.

AXIOMS AND PRINCIPLES

All inquiry begins with certain assumptions. If these are not made clear they may be explicated (with varying success) by reflective examination. But however successful our reflection turns out, we can only go so far and no farther. As we have seen, any explanatory system rests on assumptions which cannot be accounted for by the system in question. This limiting feature of explanation can be framed in terms of one basic question: how do we establish first principles? If they are truly first, then only one answer is possible: we accept them in order to get on with the business of explanation. Only on the basis of such an acceptance is any intellectual task possible.

Both classical and modern political theory, therefore, possess a noncognitive base. In Platonic philosophy the noncognitive element is accepted into the main body of the philosophy.

Then by the second section of the intelligible world you may understand me to mean all that unaided reason apprehends by the power of dialectic, when it treats its assumptions, not as first principles, but as *hypotheses* in the literal sense, things 'laid down' like a flight of steps up which it may mount all the way to something that is not hypothetical, *the first principle of all* . . .[10]

As we have seen, the highest form in Plato's stages of cognition is the Good, which is mystical, and which can only be grasped as the result of an intuitive experience. A more empirically oriented political theory will not incorporate noncognitivism so directly. But, again, empirical inquiry must itself be based on a prior principle escaping explicit validation. Hence, modern political theory also possesses an intuitive dimension.

Curiously enough, the most systematic attempt to translate all of knowing into an explicit set of rules—positivism—is predicated on a theory of value which is entirely noncognitive. The extreme nature of positivist claims has already been severely qualified. But it remains true that some form of emotivism, in the sense that value judgments ascribe favor, is always basic to any affirmation. In the case of positivism this results in the peculiar dilemma that one's theory of knowledge must be affirmed on grounds antagonistic to the same theory of knowledge. In the case of more flexible epistemologies, it means that the full understanding of what one is saying suggests an examination of noncognitive areas.

How one engages in such an undertaking is a complex subject in itself. Part of the task is recognizing that there *is* an intuitive dimension to all political inquiry. This involves rejecting the view that the study of politics is a science and nothing else. It may be a science insofar as science is defined as a factual enterprise, but what allows factual investigation to take place is a wide assortment of noncognitive beginnings. Included in these beginnings are the symbolic devices of a culture as well as the physiological bases of all social behavior.

[10] Plato, *Republic*, F. M. Cornford, ed. (New York: Oxford University Press, 1945), pp. 225–26. (Last italics added.)

Exhausting the primordial axioms of any form of inquiry is, of course, impossible. Even the most systematic scrutiny of noncognitive factors possesses its own set of assumptions. Further, where mysticism begins, intellectual discourse thins out. But, as with most things, no sharp boundary distinguishes the cognitive and noncognitive. The series of gradations separating these two dimensions of a theory include what may be taken as neither one nor the other. Myths, for example, are conceptual devices which may function as rationales for participant behavior, or intellectual direction for explanatory schemes. Attempting to understand such quasi-cognitive devices may expand the understanding of experience which is more cognitive.

The inescapable fact about any theory is that it is, in the most fundamental way, generated by the intuitive seeing of the theorist. Theories are not totally intuitive, for a useful theory must explain experience in a way that can be grasped by others. But the impetus for focusing on one thing instead of another, and the way in which we focus on experience, is not normally included in theoretical explanation itself. The problem is that what is normally included may not be enough. If what we say is truly conditioned by how we come to say it, then explanation must focus on its origins in order to insure its own validity.

EXHORTATIONS AND CONCLUSIONS

The conclusion to be drawn, finally, is that political investigation is both explanatory and ethical in character. Values are relevant as the emotive (or noncognitive) premises of all discourse, and as the prescriptive decisions made by actors. Values, therefore, are (in these two ways) the constant features of all political theory. The first area of values is connected with all social inquiry, while the second is distinctive of political analysis alone. Both point to the same conclusion: the question of evaluation must be engaged

in the study of politics. Two observations support this assertion. First, explanation itself must come to terms with its
own ethical assumptions. Second, prescriptive behavior can
only be studied as a factual instance of the general idea of
evaluation.

It cannot be emphasized too often that factual inquiry can
be predicated on any of a number of ethical premises. As
Weber has demonstrated, *after* the point of view has been
established it is possible to make factual judgments. But
the larger role of general theory in social inquiry embodies
more of the point of view, and hence more than its share of
ethical bias; for general theory includes a wide range of concepts which are not directly factual. Hence the unraveling of
the point of view within which explanation takes place is
especially crucial to a full understanding of general theories,
and more or less relevant to the validity of explanations as
such.

On this point a wide range of agreement might be expected.

> What is true of research in general is no less true of systematic
> theory. Without attempting to argue here what I have sought
> to demonstrate elsewhere, it can be said that the kind of
> variables which a theorist considers cogent for his theory, the
> type of data he selects to test it, even the kinds of relations
> he sees among his variables, normally show a significant rela-
> tion to his moral premises. In systematic theory, as in purely
> factual research, we may banish all reference to values, but
> this does not in itself prove that our ultimate preferences may
> not have exercised an unobtrusive influence on our observa-
> tions and reasoning.[11]

More rare is an agreement on the mode of examination.
Rarer still is the successful completion of such an undertaking. Two approaches to the problem of exhuming ethical

[11] David Easton, *The Political System* (New York: Alfred A. Knopf,
1959), p. 227.

premises have already been rejected. One is the construction of an ideal state. The other is the set of choices which an individual will make in an ultimate situation.[12] The antithesis of these dual attempts, or the assertion that we are hopelessly biased, has also been discarded.

One way of getting at the noncognitive beginnings of all inquiry is by focusing on the epistemologies of political theories. By analyzing the meanings and uses of political concepts we get at the fundamental way in which politics is experienced and, also, at the ethical foundations of our inquiry. This means that the empirical emphasis in political analysis must be supplemented with a philosophical analysis of the concepts tested. It is natural to suppose that, since empirical investigation cannot be conducted without a conceptual scheme, the conceptual scheme is also a fair topic for systematic study.

But epistemology does not adequately get at the continuing exchanges between theory and phenomena, nor at the origins of our theories in experience. Another approach to these problems is itself empirical, although with a specified focus: the investigation of politics can also be directed at the process of political socialization, or how we come to be political creatures in the first place. This would mean studying the way in which children assume the cognitive and evaluative concepts which go into the making of political experience.[13] By focusing on this process the noncognitive origins of theories (which include their deepest ethical premises) might be more fully explicated than in any purely epistemological exercise.

A study of socialization may be combined successfully

[12] *Ibid.*, pp. 229–32. See discussion in Chapter V.

[13] One interesting study along these lines is David Easton and Robert Hess, "The Child's Political World," in the *Midwest Journal of Political Science* (August 1962), pp. 229–46. Also see David Easton and Jack Dennis, "The Child's Acquisition of Regime Norms: Political Efficacy," *American Political Science Review*, LXI (March 1967), pp. 25–38.

with the analysis of political symbols and their meaning for the individuals embracing them. The norm of rational behavior does not, finally, account for the mythical or intuitive nature of much political behavior. A study of irrational devices must rely on the relationship of unconscious to conscious behavior, and not simply on the analytic norm of rationality. When combined with the continuity between physiological and conscious behavior,[14] the picture becomes even more complete. The efficacy of such an undertaking is basic, for by focusing on the noncognitive foundation of explanation the explicit distinctions between classical rationalism and modern empiricism may be submerged within a larger question: how one assumes basic sets of categories in accounting for experience. In this way we also get at the cultural framework within which explanation must take place.

Many of these suggestions are merely observations about work which is already taking place. Others are not. But they add up to a proposal at variance with the primary intent of modern political analysis, for what is suggested here is not another factual theory for explaining the ongoing polity. It is, rather, a proposal for examining how it is we can explain politics at all; or, as analogous to the Kantian a priori, what are suggested here as an important focus for political inquiry are those factors in the absence of which political experience would not be possible.

From the second of the normative considerations a more standard inference can be drawn, although one which still

[14] Ethology may be a relevant inclusion. See, for example, Konrad Lorenz's *On Aggression* (New York: Harcourt, Brace & World, 1966). The way in which noncognitive beginnings yield to cognitive experience might even make possible the establishment of a general relationship between physiological and psychological variables in political theory. Hence, the work currently being done by Jerome Bruner on the study of children in precognitive and cognitive stages of growth is especially important. See Bruner's *Toward a Theory of Instruction* (Cambridge, Mass.: Harvard University Press, 1966).

suggests a new emphasis in political analysis. If the focus of all political investigation is on prescriptive behavior, then an empirical theory of evaluation is of prime necessity for the study of politics. The development of such a theory would include the establishment of factual generalizations about the way in which actors make value judgments in differing situations. But it would also include an explication of what evaluation means in a political setting. As with the development of any theory, both data and conceptual apparatus are appropriate foci for analysis.

On the separate question of recommendations in any general theory of value, little need be added. Actors make value judgments. Political analysts can also, even though judgments are not logical derivations from facts. The abrasive fit of facts and values has been overly emphasized too long. It is the stuff of politics to prescribe norms. To deny that the political analyst can do so is to misrepresent a logician's dilemma. Political inquiry is an instrument to make sense of the political world, and one way of doing this is to tie together the cognitive and evaluative approaches to politics. Plato's tight connection of expertise and values may be dead, but a looser relationship between what we know and how we value has already been demonstrated in this work. The polity is the highest form of normative order. To let it pass without normative comment can only be cavalier.

Selected Bibliography

BOOKS

ALMOND, GABRIEL, *et al. Politics of the Developing Areas.* Princeton: Princeton University Press, 1960.

———, AND POWELL, G. BINGHAM, JR. *Comparative Politics: A Developmental Approach.* Boston: Little, Brown, and Company, 1966.

ARISTOTLE. *Ethics.* Translated by J. A. K. Thomson. Baltimore: Penguin Books, 1953.

———. *Politics.* Translated by Ernest Barker. New York: Oxford University Press, 1946.

AYER, A. J. *Language, Truth, and Logic.* New York: Dover Publications, 1946.

BARKER, ERNEST. *Greek Political Theory.* New York: Barnes and Noble, 1960.

BENDIX, RICHARD. *Max Weber.* New York: Doubleday and Company, 1960.

BLALOCK, HUBERT M. *Causal Inferences in Nonexperimental Research.* Chapel Hill: University of North Carolina Press, 1961.

BRECHT, ARNOLD. *Political Theory.* Princeton: Princeton University Press, 1959.

CAMPBELL, ANGUS, *et al. The American Voter.* New York: John Wiley & Sons, 1960.

CAMUS, ALBERT. *The Myth of Sisyphus.* New York: Vintage Books, 1959.

CHARLESWORTH, JAMES C. (ed.). *A Design for Political Science.* Philadelphia: The American Academy of Political and Social Science, 1966.

COLLINGWOOD, R. G. *The Idea of Nature.* New York: Oxford University Press, 1960.

CONANT, JAMES. *Science and Common Sense*. New Haven: Yale University Press, 1951.

COPLESTON, FREDERICK. *History of Philosophy*. Vol. I: *Greece and Rome*. Westminster, Maryland: The Newman Press, 1963.

————. *Contemporary Philosophy*. Westminster, Maryland: The Newman Press, 1956.

CORNFORD, FRANCIS M. *Before and After Socrates*. Cambridge: Cambridge University Press, 1962.

————. *Plato's Theory of Knowledge*. New York: Bobbs-Merrill, 1957.

DAHL, ROBERT. *Modern Political Analysis*. Englewood Cliffs, N.J.: Prentice-Hall, 1963.

DEWEY, JOHN. *Theory of Valuation*. Chicago: University of Chicago Press, 1939.

DOWNS, ANTHONY. *An Economic Theory of Democracy*. New York: Harper and Row, 1957.

EASTON, DAVID. *A Framework for Political Analysis*. Englewood Cliffs, N.J.: Prentice-Hall, 1965.

————. *The Political System*. New York: Alfred E. Knopf, 1953.

————. *A Systems Analysis of Political Life*. New York: John Wiley & Sons, 1965.

EDELMAN, MURRAY. *The Symbolic Uses of Politics*. Urbana: University of Illinois Press, 1964.

FESTINGER, LEON, AND KATZ, DANIEL. *Research Methods in the Behavioral Sciences*. New York: The Dryden Press, 1953.

GERTH, H. H., AND MILLS, C. WRIGHT. *From Max Weber*. New York: Oxford University Press, 1958.

GIBSON, QUENTIN. *The Logic of Social Inquiry*. New York: The Humanities Press, 1959.

GROSS, LLEWELLYN (ed.). *Symposium on Sociological Theory*. New York: Harper and Row, 1959.

GUTHRIE, W. K. C. *The Greek Philosophers*. New York: Harper and Row, 1960.

HART, HERBERT LIONEL ADOLPHUS. *The Concept of Law*. Oxford: Clarendon Press, 1961.

HEMPEL, CARL. *Fundamentals of Concept Formation in Empirical Science*. Chicago: University of Chicago Press, 1952.

HUME, DAVID. *An Inquiry Concerning the Principles of Morals*. New York: The Liberal Arts Press, 1957.

HYMAN, HERBERT. *Survey Design and Analysis*. Glencoe: The Free Press, 1954.

KAPLAN, ABRAHAM. *The Conduct of Inquiry*. San Francisco: Chandler Publishing Co., 1964.

KOHLER, WOLFGANG. *Gestalt Psychology*. New York: H. Liveright, 1929.

————. *The Place of Value in a World of Fact*. New York: Meridian Books, 1959.

KUHN, THOMAS. *The Structure of Scientific Revolutions*. Chicago: University of Chicago Press, 1962.

LANE, ROBERT. *Political Ideology*. Glencoe: The Free Press, 1962.

MANNHEIM, KARL. *Ideology and Utopia*. New York: Harcourt, Brace and Company, 1936.

MASLOW, A. H. *Motivation and Personality*. New York: Harper, 1954.

MERTON, ROBERT. *Social Theory and Social Structure*. Glencoe: The Free Press, 1957.

MOORE, G. E. *Philosophical Studies*. London: Routledge and Kegan Paul Ltd., 1922.

————. *Principia Ethica*. Cambridge: Cambridge University Press, 1962.

MYRDAL, GUNNAR. *Value in Social Theory*. Edited by Paul Streeten. New York: Harper and Row, 1958.

NAGEL, ERNEST. *The Structure of Science*. New York: Harcourt, Brace and World, 1961.

NATANSON, MAURICE. *Literature, Philosophy, and the Social Sciences*. The Hague: Martinus Nijhoff, 1962.

————. (ed.). *The Philosophy of the Social Sciences*. New York: Random House, 1963.

PAP, ARTHUR. *Introduction to the Philosophy of Science*. Glencoe: The Free Press, 1962.

PARSONS, TALCOTT. *The Structure of Social Action.* Glencoe: The Free Press, 1949.

————, AND SHILS, EDWARD (eds.). *Toward a General Theory of Action.* New York: Harper and Row, 1962.

PLATO. *The Dialogues of Plato.* Vols. I and II. Translated by B. Jowett. New York: Random House, 1937.

————. *Gorgias.* Translated by W. Hamilton. Baltimore: Penguin Books, 1960.

————. *Protagoras and Meno.* Translated by W. K. C. Guthrie. Baltimore: Penguin Books, 1956.

————. *Republic.* Translated by Francis Cornford. New York: Oxford University Press, 1945.

POLANYI, MICHAEL. *Personal Knowledge.* Chicago: University of Chicago Press, 1958.

————. *Science, Faith, and Society.* Chicago: University of Chicago Press, 1964.

————. Unpublished Lectures at Duke University. Spring, 1964.

POPPER, KARL. *The Logic of Scientific Discovery.* New York: Harper and Row, 1959.

RANDALL, JOHN. *Aristotle.* New York: Columbia University Press, 1960.

REICHENBACH, HANS. *The Rise of Scientific Philosophy.* Berkeley: University of California Press, 1964.

ROSS, W. D. *Aristotle.* New York: Meridian Books, 1959.

RUDNER, RICHARD. *Philosophy of Social Science.* Englewood Cliffs, N.J.: Prentice-Hall, 1966.

RUNCIMAN, W. G. *Social Science and Political Theory.* Cambridge: Cambridge University Press, 1963.

RYLE, GILBERT. *The Concept of Mind.* New York: Barnes and Noble, 1949.

SELLARS, WILFRED, AND HOSPERS, JOHN (eds.). *Readings in Ethical Theory.* New York: Appleton-Century-Crofts, Inc., 1952.

STRAUSS, LEO. *Natural Right and History.* Chicago: University of Chicago Press, 1953.

————. *What is Political Philosophy?* Glencoe: The Free Press, 1959.

TAYLOR, A. E. *Plato.* New York: Meridian Books, 1956.

————. *Socrates.* New York: Doubleday and Company, 1952.

TOULMIN, STEPHEN. *The Philosophy of Science.* New York: Harper and Row, 1960.

————. *Reason in Ethics.* Cambridge: Cambridge University Press, 1960.

ULMER, S. SIDNEY (ed.). *Introductory Readings in Political Behavior.* Chicago: Rand McNally, 1961.

VOEGELIN, ERIC. *The New Science of Politics.* Chicago: University of Chicago Press, 1952.

————. *Plato and Aristotle.* Baton Rouge: Louisiana State University Press, 1957.

WEBER, MAX. *Basic Concepts in Sociology.* Translated by H. P. Secher. New York: The Citadel Press, 1963.

————. *The Methodology of the Social Sciences.* Glencoe: The Free Press, 1949.

————. *The Theory of Social and Economic Organization.* Translated by A. M. Henderson and Talcott Parsons. Glencoe: The Free Press, 1964.

WEIGEL, GUSTAVE, AND MADDEN, ARTHUR G. *Knowledge: Its Values and Limits.* Englewood Cliffs, N.J.: Prentice-Hall, 1961.

WELDON, T. D. *The Vocabulary of Politics.* Baltimore: Penguin Books, 1953.

WINCH, PETER. *The Idea of a Social Science.* New York: Humanities Press, 1958.

WOLIN, SHELDON. *Politics and Vision.* Boston: Little, Brown, and Co., 1960.

YOUNG, ROLAND. (ed.). *Approaches to the Study of Politics.* Evanston: Northwestern University Press, 1958.

ARTICLES

BAY, CHRISTIAN. "Politics and PseudoPolitics," *American Political Science Review*, LIX (March, 1965), 39–51.

BLALOCK, H., AND BLALOCK, A.   "Toward a Clarification of Systems Analysis in the Social Sciences," *Philosophy of Science,* XXVI (April, 1959), 84–92.

BLAU, PETER.   "Critical Remarks on Weber's Theory of Authority," *American Political Science Review,* LVII (June, 1963), 305–16.

BRUNER, JEROME S., AND POSTMAN, LEE.   "On the Perception of Incongruity: A Paradigm," *Journal of Personality,* XVII (1949-1950), 206–23.

DOWSE, ROBERT.   "A Functionalist's Logic," *World Politics,* XVIII (July, 1966), 607–22.

EASTON, DAVID, AND HESS, ROBERT.   "The Child's Political World," *Midwest Journal of Political Science,* VI (August, 1962), 229–46.

FULLER, LON.   "Human Purpose and Natural Law," *Natural Law Forum,* III (1958), 68–76.

————.   "A Rejoinder to Professor Nagel," *Natural Law Forum,* III (1958), 83–104.

FURFEY, PAUL H.   "Metasociological Value Judgments," *The Scope and Method of Sociology.* Chapter IV. New York: Harper and Brothers, 1953, pp. 87–106.

HALLOWELL, JOHN.   "Politics and Ethics," *American Political Science Review,* XXXVIII (August, 1944), 639–55.

MITCHELL, WILLIAM.   "Politics as the Allocation of Values: A Critique," *Ethics,* LXXI (January, 1961), 79–89.

NAGEL, ERNEST.   "Fact, Value, and Human Purpose," *Natural Law Forum,* IV (1959), 26–43.

————.   "On the Fusion of Fact and Value: A Reply to Professor Fuller," *Natural Law Forum,* III (1958), 77–82.

————.   "Problems of Concept and Theory Formation in the Social Sciences," *Science, Language, and Human Rights.* Philadelphia: University of Pennsylvania Press, 1952, pp. 43–64.

POLANYI, MICHAEL.   "The Logic of Tacit Inference," *Philosophy,* XLI (January, 1966), 1–18.

RAPOPORT, ANATOL.   "The Various Meanings of Theory," *American Political Science Review,* LII (December, 1958), 972–88.

REID, JOHN.   "The Nature and Status of Values," in *Philosophy for the Future*. Edited by Roy Sellars, V. J. McGill, and Marvin Farber. New York: The MacMillan Company, 1949, pp. 453–75.

TRUMAN, DAVID.   "Disillusion and Regeneration: The Quest for a Discipline," *American Political Science Review*, LIX (December, 1965), 865–73.

VAN DYKE, VERNON.   "Values and Interests," *American Political Science Review*, LVI (September, 1962), 567–76.

WILD, JOHN.   "Natural Law and Modern Ethical Theory," *Ethics*, LXIII (October, 1952), 1–13.

Index of Names

Index of Subjects

This book has been set in 11 and 10 point Caledonia, leaded 2 points. Chapter numbers are in 14 point Venus Medium Extended; chapter titles are in 18 point Venus Medium Extended. The size of the type page is 24 by 40⅔ picas.